Seven Perfect Marriages That Failed

Seven Perfect Marriages That Failed

SUSAN HAVEN and DANIEL KLEIN

STEIN AND DAY/*Publishers*/New York

First published in 1975
Copyright © 1975 by Susan Haven and Daniel Klein
All rights reserved
Designed by David Miller
Printed in the United States of America
Stein and Day/*Publishers*/Scarborough House,
Briarcliff Manor, N.Y. 10510

Library of Congress Cataloging in Publication Data

Haven, Susan.
    Seven perfect marriages that failed.

    1.   Marriage—United States—Case studies. I. Klein, Daniel,
joint author. II. Title.
HQ536.H36   301.42'0973   74-28077
ISBN 0-8128-1777-X

Love is an ideal thing, marriage a real thing; a confusion of the real with the ideal never goes unpunished.

—GOETHE

Contents

1

Introduction

Jeff and Nora were a perfect couple—perfectly matched and perfectly in love. Everybody could see they were soul mates. In 1965 they married. In 1972 they divorced.

This is a book of love stories with tragic endings. They are true stories, told by couples who seemed to be ideal mates, whose love appeared truer and luckier than most others, who seemed to have perfect marriages—and who finally had to end them. Each of these marriages was actually two marriages—his and hers—and both stories are told, side by side. It is a book of marital who-done-its, an attempt to discover why these marriages did not and, in fact, could not succeed.

Each of these couples acted out a tantalizing myth of perfect marriage:

The Super Achievers—the glamorous pair with power and fame who seemed destined to master the world together;

The Super Erotics—the couple who felt they were ideally suited to lead one another to the highest peaks of sexual satisfaction;

The Worshiper and the Worshipee—the loving team who shared the understanding that she would provide him with comfort and emotional support and he would provide her with stability, strength, and worldly success;

The Spiritual Couple—the pair who shared transcendental values and joined together on their quest for a pure, spiritual life;

The Soul Mates—the lovers who considered themselves the unique complements to one another and who were welded together by an intense intellectual intimacy;

The Simple Nesters—the couple who shared the picturesque dream of a warm home, cheerful children, and strong family spirit;

And the Open Marriage Couple—the pair who loved and respected each other's independence and together planned each other's growth.

In an age when most people are demanding more than ever before from marriage, the perfect-marriage myths these seven couples illustrate are particularly seductive. Each myth promises a marriage with deeper feelings, more fulfilling experiences, and a superior life-style: A perfect marriage would satisfy every aspiration.

But in fact we are surrounded by perfect marriages that fail. Why? Is there something in the myths that can destroy a marriage? Do these myths set up impossible standards, contradictory goals, and dreams that go beyond the limits of anybody's nervous system? By aspiring to perfect marriage, are couples helping to save marriage or are they really aspiring to disaster? This book was written in the hope that an exploration of perfect marriages that have failed will provide clues to what *real* marriage can be.

In surveying perfect marriages that failed, we saw certain myths cropping up repeatedly. Each of the stories chosen for this book best exemplified one of the most prevalent myths. There are elements of several myths in each of these marriages—as in most marriages—but one is always dominant.

All interviews were made separately, our woman partner interviewing the former wives and our man partner interviewing the former husbands. For in addition to the perfect-marriage myth each couple shared, each man and woman came away from their marriage with dramatically different ideas of what went on. This book presents both stories with no attempt to blame either mate. The names and other identifying characteristics of the people interviewed were, of course, changed for publication.

In presenting the narratives of these perfect marriages, we made every effort to bring out a true and complete story. Distilling a narrative inevitably simplifies it, but if we brought any special focus to this project, it was our curiosity about how myths operated in the marriages. When reading these stories, look for the effects of the myths. Was it a mythical goal that ruined a couple's sex life? A fantasy aspiration that made a mate seem boring? Did some ideal—either traditional or recently developed—of what a man or woman should be make the marriage unendurable? Certain words appear repeatedly in these narratives—words like "depth," "passion," "spontaneity," "growth," "change," "bohemian," "wanderer." They are all part of the vocabulary of the myth of perfect marriage.

Our belief is not that all perfect marriages must fail, but that the myths of our culture have put a terrible, often impossible strain on marriage. The couples who have attempted to live out the myths of perfect marriage are the groundbreakers for all of us. They are the idealists and experimenters from whom we all learn. We are deeply grateful to the people who so openly shared with us the intimate stories of their marriages.

SOPHIA AND ROBERT
Chronology

1960	Robert's and Sophia's first date.
August, 1961	They are engaged.
July, 1962	They marry.
1963	They spend a year in Europe.
1964	Robert is employed by R. Thornton, a major architectural firm in New York.
1965	Sophia is made fashion editor of a major magazine.
1966	Billy is born.
1968	Robert starts his own architectural office.
1971	Sophia quits her job and begins to paint.
October, 1972	They separate briefly.
October, 1973	Last separation.

2

The
Super Achievers

The Super Achievers marriage myth features the fondest American dream: the dream of glamour and success. This is the wedding of two masterful people who know how to live with style and verve. They pursue independent careers that bring each of them power, recognition, and international mobility, and they bring the best of their worlds to one another. They regard each other with pride and everyone else regards the two of them with awe. They are, indeed, the Golden Couple.

Robert and Sophia Hobson came to their marriage with sophisticated backgrounds and high goals. Together, they quickly reached the tops of their fields.

Tall and attractive with her modellike figure and curly black hair, Sophia Rostov Hobson makes an impressive appearance. She dresses simply but fashionably and moves with grace. She is spirited and charming. Now thirty-six, Sophia earns a living as a free-lance fashion consultant and also paints. She lives with her son Billy, nine, in a loft in the SoHo district of New York.

SOPHIA:

I left Vassar in 1960 and lived in New York with my friend Winnie Sloan of the Harrison Scott Sloans, if you can remember them. We lived on Sullivan Street; I wanted to be a writer and she wanted to be a poet. I don't know exactly how it happened, but I became a copywriter. I somehow confused the two. I was going out with a lot of people, including a friend of Rob's from Chicago. So one night Rob called me and said, "Listen, my friend John Thatcher had such a good time with you, I'd like to go out with you." So fine. He said there was a concert at Sarah Lawrence this weekend and he knew I went to Short Hills on the weekend and he lived in Upper Montclair and would I like to go? So I said, "Yes, if I may."

I met him at my parents' house. I had on a tweed skirt and a pair of sneakers with no socks. I said, "Look, do you mind these sneakers with no socks?" And he said that maybe I should put on a pair of regular shoes. That irked me a little, but he was very attractive, very Ivy League, so he was all right. He took me to dinner at this charming place. He was very sophisticated and I liked this a lot. I wanted to see him again.

He made one remark that made me want to see him more and more. He said that he often went to the Museum of Modern Art. He was the only person I had met that had any genuine interest in the arts, other than my parents and a couple of girls I knew who seemed kind of creepy. All my other friends from Vassar were only interested in boys, money, and getting married.

Another thing about Rob was that he was very reserved. I found that attractive. I mean, psychologically, I like someone who is quiet, which I am not. In our relationship, I always felt that I was the charming, outgoing one. And he was very quiet. I was never ashamed of him, but I always felt that the eyes were on me. Actually I dislike charm, especially in the way I was using it then—but I had it and I could turn it on and off at will.

We were going out together frequently. I was a virgin at the time. This is just so typical of those days. I decided, This is it: I've got to lose my virginity somewhere. So we had sexual relations. They were OK. They were good, I guess. I mean, how did I know? It wasn't passion that attracted me to him. It was a warm, comforting kind of thing. He is so reliable. You just tell him and he does it. And nice, he is the nicest person I know. This guy was really a gem.

Somewhere along the line I had the feeling that if I didn't marry him, he would go his way and I would never find anybody so right again that I liked as much. I was just crazy about him. If you meet Rob, you see immediately he's a perfectionist. Exquisite taste. I mean, he's a tastemaker.

We went to my parents and told them that we were getting married and my parents said, "Absolutely not. You can't marry him." Well, I was knocked through a loop. They said, "We will disown you. We don't want to see you again." I couldn't understand why they weren't overjoyed. Rob was everything that they ever wanted. This guy is as solid as the Gibraltar Rock. I was just so shocked that I didn't register it. We went home in his car and I said that they're just sort of stunned.

But they persisted. My mother came to my office and started crying and said, "If you marry him, I'll die." I said, "Why?" And she said, "We just don't think he's right for you." Finally they said that they were sure Rob was Jewish, of all things, and, "We don't want you to marry somebody Jewish." My parents are raging liberals—quote—the raging liberals of Short Hills (laughs). So I went to this woman who was a lay analyst and she said, "Marry him and they will do a turnabout and love him." And sure enough, when I got married, my parents did an about-face. We could do no wrong. They loved him more than they loved me.

I'd always wanted to go to Europe. And he said, "Okay.

I'll go too." He's very, very flexible. Underneath, and I learned this later, he doesn't always mean it. But we went to Europe and we had a superb trip. We faced it all together—all the new things, all the unknown things. We learned about food. We learned about wine. I began really to respect this guy even more. When we got into a city, he would look up the institute of architects, find out the major architects there, call them up at their offices, make appointments to see them, and eleven years later, this whole thing came into fruition because he is working with people in Europe that he met on that trip.

That year there was something to do every minute. We went to Portugal and had one magical week on a beach. We went to Spain where places were $1.50 a day with great food, great wine. It was before the whole world became insanely expensive. And Rob was always wanting to push on because there were always new contacts and new adventures. But I prevailed on him—"Let's stay here." And we stayed for ten days in Spain and lived on the beach. In this Spanish interlude, we met the most charming vagabond people like ourselves. We'd always meet them wherever we were. And we talked incessantly, if not communicating feelings and caring for each other, about environment and at least intellectual things. We were utterly alone for a year. And if you don't get a divorce after a year in a Volkswagen—we thought we were golden forever. Those were really halcyon days.

Then we came back to the harsh realities of life. Rob got a job with Roger Thornton, a leading architect, and I went back to my job at the magazine. Rob began sliding into a different value system, and I'm drawn into all of this physicality around me. The beautiful. He brings beautiful plants home and everything is just so. He buys this stainless-steel furniture and I say, "That's just great." And I think to myself, Well, I don't really like stainless steel. But he gets the stainless-steel furniture and I say that I like it even better than he does. He brought wines home. We had wonderful wine-tasting evenings, and I'd cook these superb dinners with wine. Those were beautiful times. Just the two of us. I'd get flowers—just for us—flowers and food and wine. We would be in heaven. We liked ourselves hugely.

I liked fashion because I like the style of everything. Rob's life was based on style, and mine too. I love clothes—only recently can I admit that. I was made fashion editor, with a great deal of power under the editor in chief, and it was going to my head. And then they said, We want you to be editor in chief. We were sought after for dinner parties and things like that. Rob is exuding this feeling of "I'm the best in my field," and people are very interested in him. I felt that was very important. We had every material thing I ever wanted. I had beautiful trips to Europe three times a year from the magazine. When we were home, I was entertaining with little tables with bouquets on them and making eggs with gelatin and truffles. I was doing television shows and all of that stuff, functioning very well. But I was really unhappy. The higher I was, the unhappier I was getting.

Meanwhile, Rob wants a child. Badly. So he's sort of after me and I say, "Oh . . . no." But I'm using no birth control at all and letting the chips fall where they may. I don't think anything is going to happen, but it's a good way to say, "All right." One day I got desperately ill. I say, "Rob, I'm dying. I'm really sick." He hauled me to the doctor, who gave me every test under the sun. Finally, the doctor says, "Do you think you're pregnant?" And I say, "Absolutely not." I'm convinced I have cancer of the stomach. They said every test was negative, but the pregnancy test was positive. I thought it was all psychological. Anyway, I had this adorable child and immediately hired a nurse. In fact, I'm back at work six days after he was born.

Life was veiled in those years by the fact that we thought ourselves so wonderful. Like this trip to Paris we took a few years ago was one of the most memorable experiences of my life. We knew lots of people in Paris by then. We were very sophisticated. We had piles of dough, beautiful clothes, superb luggage. We knew where to go. We were the total opposite of what we had been ten years ago—ten years ago we didn't know anything about superb luggage. We lived in the Ritz. The bathroom was as big as a living room and all in marble. They would bring us breakfast every morning with exquisite china and flowers, beautiful shapes. The sheets were changed every day. We ordered a bottle of Perrier water and it would come up in a champagne bucket with champagne glasses. We'd sit there just smug as hell and drink water. We wanted to be fat cats. It was just the two of us again and each time we have operated as two people together in a strange environment, we've been terribly successful. It's when we were in our own environments that we tended to go against each other.

Oh yes, we were so marvelous, but a part of me knew it was a sham. Rob never thought so. In one sense he was right—he was a successful architect. But the sham for Rob was that he never felt that he was unhappy. I knew he was. Rob now knows it too. I don't know which is better. I was always unhappy somewhere and I considered it neurotic. Once I had three dreams in rapid succession of self-destruction, and the message was that I'm not headed in the right direction and I thought I'd better see a psychiatrist. I went to this lay analyst and he was very tweedy. He was not an MD and he only asked me about menstrual cycles. I said, "This is not my problem," and left.

But a significant thing had happened to me in the meantime. I had been working very closely with a whole lot of photographers. The fashion world is very incestuous and very physical. The whole life is sensuality and sex and people are having affairs all over. The idea of having any relationships outside of my marriage never—literally never—occurred to me because all I was thinking about was making money and being the editor in chief and writing.

Then I went down to Florida on a shooting with this photographer I had sort of been fascinated by and we had some sort of a fashiony thing together and he says to me very wisely, "I don't want to get involved with you. You're married and I think you should see a doctor because I think you're too unhappy." So I take his advice and I start seeing another doctor. This is number three. It's a woman psychiatrist and her name is Dr. Fellows. All we talked about was dreams, only dream life. Finally one day I said, "Look, nothing of this is relating to reality. I can't make the jump from this office to what is going on in my life."

I came home crying every day and I'd say to Rob, "This life is terrible. I can't stand it." I'd say to him, "You're not cool, you're uptight. You never do anything but your design and polishing your car. You don't have any hobbies or friends. Why don't you learn to cook? Why don't you take me to a poetry reading? Why don't you learn the names of plants? You're boring. You're bumbling." Now for somebody to tell you you're boring is devastating. And this guy took that for about five years. In truth, he *was* boring.

I remember one evening I disliked Rob so intensely. We had a woman named Regina over for dinner. At that time she was an editor of *Vogue*. She had gone to Sarah Lawrence and I had gone to Vassar, which doesn't mean anything except that we could talk about subjects other than the clothes on one's back and the Estée Lauder beauty creams. She's opinionated and ve-rr-y bright. A very impressive personality. She had been married to this prominent writer and lived for years with a famous director. I wanted her to like me and I wanted her to like Rob. I cooked a nice dinner, pasta of some sort, and we sat around afterward and talked about sophistication and culture. We got onto the subject of the Eskimos and African tribes, and the level of their culture. Rob got onto the point of view that their culture was far more advanced than Western or Eastern cultures. We were talking about stuff he did not know about and he would not stop. He eventually put himself into a position where he had to defend something outrageous. I was so angry.

There was one saving grace in the whole conversation that I really did like him for, though. We were talking about the craftsmanship of the Eskimos and he said that he considered himself an "artisan craftsman" on the highest level. I thought that was a superb way of putting his whole personality. But basically I felt Regina thought what a stupid pain he was and how could Sophia be married to somebody so stupid.

Finally, one night I said to Rob, "Let's get out. Let's live downtown. Let's get a loft and you paint. I will work and support you at whatever you want to do. I don't think I want to do anything, but I can't live this constipated life any longer." He said, "Okay." So I say, "There's a friend of yours, Tom, we met ten years ago who had a loft downtown. Call him up and see if he knows of any lofts available." Rob called him and asked him for dinner. Tom comes up and, well, I have never felt a passion like that in my life for a guy. Just like that. And it was sort of returned. There was no loft available and I was going to come downtown and look. I called Tom up two days later and from that time on there really hasn't been a day I haven't seen him.

Meanwhile Rob and I are seeing a doctor that this Dr. Fellows recommends, a marriage counselor. And this doctor says to me, "You are the most arrogant, elitist woman I have ever met. And this poor guy, Rob, you're taking him for all he's worth." And I'm thinking, I really am. I'm having an affair with somebody else and there's something terribly, terribly wrong. So I say to Rob, "I don't want to see this doctor anymore." And Rob says, "Okay, then you see a doctor and I'll see a doctor." And I said, "This is like *New York Magazine*. It's such a typical article, I can't stand it!"

But I went to see another doctor. This is a doctor's doctor, one of the most eminent doctors in the city. He said to me, "You're basically having an identity problem. You don't know who you are." And I thought, "You're right. I don't know who I am, but please help me." And nobody was helping me, except Tom.

I just wanted to be with Tom. I wanted to have his way of life. He had no responsibilities. He paid eighty dollars a month rent. My biggest beef with Rob was, "You don't feel deeply! I need that quality of depth of feeling. You have a horizontal kind of thinking." Tom has depth. He really understands what's going on.

So I'm wandering around in a morass; nothing is real. There is Billy, who is a tremendous responsibility. There's Rob, who is always very nice, but who says, "You're very sick," in his nice way. I'm making money and I'm functioning and everything, but I can't take it. I quit the job and I decide I'm going to free-lance and be a painter. Tom became my teacher. In a sense, he was my teacher about passion too. Every day for two years I went to Tom's. And then one day in 1973 I went down to Rob's office and I said, "I'm leaving you." Just like that. There was no preface, no warning, nothing. I said, "I'm going off to live with Tom." Well, at this point my poor husband, I mean, he just turned white. He said, "You'll never have a job again. I'll crucify your existence."

So I went down to live with Tom for two days and Tom is a real bastard. He lives in a pigsty. I can't stand it. You know, you can love somebody, but you can't live with him. He doesn't take a bath. I said to Rob, "I can't stand Tom," and Rob said, "Come back and we'll try and work things out." I do and I go back to Dr. Fellows and she says, "You've got to try harder if you want your marriage to work." I'm thinking I'm a real mental case, that I'm very sick. I'm thinking this because everybody keeps saying, "Sophie, you're very, very sick." So I went to a new doctor and he says, "Can't you see that it might be somebody else's problem? What about Rob?" And I said, "Rob is the biggest mass of gray that I have ever encountered in my life." Then I knew I just had to get out.

"I'm seeing Tom now and I still see Rob. I think both of them are halves of me. I'm very split in just that way. Rob is the conventional person; he does everything to a proper turn. And Tom is a true bohemian person. He doesn't give a shit about authority; he's very passionate, unhappy and happy. I have let loose with enormous emotions with Tom. It comes out at him and with him and it still frightens me enormously. I am just getting into a state of shock at the amount of rage or the amount of sexual passion that comes out of me. I hope they can be put to use fruitfully in some creative work. But I know I can't live with Tom. I can't live that insecure kind of life. I have this unforgivable trait that I like to live well. I like the clothes ironed, I like the place spick-and-span. It's uncanny, Rob and Tom represent both sides of myself and they are the people who know me best.

But it's funny, my brother and a couple of very good friends of mine say that Rob and Tom are almost interchangeable. They look alike and act alike, they both went to the same school, they're the same age. One is a painter and one an architect. They both have the same aesthetics. Superficially, it's true. But down deep, you see, my real wish is that Rob could be Tom.

I remember one of the doctors said to me, "You're just acting out," and I was very resentful of that. I hate that term, anyway. It's called living, that's all. The truth is, it was my fantasy to work in the fish market. It is my fantasy to live in a loft. It is my fantasy to be a painter. It's more than a fantasy. It's what I think is the most wonderful dream. To be a painter and live sort of a gutsy life and enjoy food and wine and friends coming by. I'm going to do what I can to make it real. And I have no regrets about it, even if I have to work myself to the bone. I think these last years have been terribly hard, but it's paid off. I won't go to my grave saying, "If I'd only done that." I *have* done that. And you know, I think Rob thinks I have a lot of guts. I wish he would think so. To me what I'm living in now is comfort. It's as rich as I'd ever want to be, but I have to struggle to maintain it.

Robert Hobson is slim, fair-haired, and neat-featured. His apartment, his furniture, his casual clothing reflect a refined taste. He has a warm, quiet manner. At thirty-nine, Robert is a highly paid and internationally known architect. He lives alone in New York City.

ROBERT:
The first time I saw Sophie was in Short Hills, when I picked her up at her folks' place for a party in Upper Montclair. She had a great speaking voice over the phone, very sexy, and I had this image of what she was going to look like: very blond, and I didn't particularly like blond ladies. So I went and met her at her house and she's a dark, very attractive lady. We went to this party and ironically we both knew all of these people who were there—basically, Vassar and Dartmouth people. It certainly was not love at first sight, but she was a very fun person to be with, a very nice lady to talk to—that came out within the first five minutes.

We saw each other in New Jersey a few times, and then I started seeing her quite frequently in New York. She was bright, responsive, very different from me. She was intellectual and I was more aesthetically oriented. She introduced me to a lot of things in music and literature.

We became lovers reasonably early, certainly after the first six times that we'd been out. And she was a virgin, which came as a huge surprise to me. We had been going through the normal out-in-the-car things, you know, kind of backwoods operations *(laughs)*. But Sophie was in the process of being very much involved—it sounds so timid now—with D. H. Lawrence at the time, and she felt experimental. So Lawrence and I shared that first experience, and it was my only bisexual experience *(laughs)*.

I called her quite early the next morning to see if she was all right. I wanted to assure her that I was not some cad that had just screwed her for the fun of it, and that was not going to be the last time just because I caught her in the spirit. From that time on we spent a lot of time together—much of it in bed, to my delight.

Soon the idea was implanted in my mind to find out whether Sophie was someone I wanted to marry. My love feelings were in the right place, but I knew I was capable of loving a lot of people, that I had loved other people before. So I was very pragmatic about marriage and I saw that Sophie was definitely a suitable wife for Robert Hobson. She fit. You know, having established certain feelings of what I wanted from a marriage, I could see pretty clearly that Sophia and I would have that. She had a very engaging style, great verve and animation, which I like enormously in a woman. And she is a very broadly knowledgeable person too. I mean, I could almost stand there at parties with my drink in hand and cock one leg out and let her go!

Whenever one of our parents went away, we would surreptitiously go to their house and stay there. We would do all the things that married people do—have friends over, give parties, eat, screw, go through a normal life's pattern for a few days at a time. Play house *(laughs)*.

One evening John and Mary came over as they often did. We'd get together and do a lot of drinking. They'd go off into a bedroom and screw for a while and Sophie and I would either do the same thing or make out on the couch. So that evening, as I recall, they both left very drunk and we were pretty done-in too. Just sitting on the couch, very drunk, but in a very sober way, I asked Sophie if she'd like to be Mrs. Hobson. She was outwardly taken by surprise and I think she said, "I'll have to think about it." And I said, "Fine. There's no rush. All the time in the world." I probably passed out at that point *(laughs)*.

I think the next day she asked me whether I remembered asking her, and I said, "Definitely. Still stands." So about two weeks passed and she called me on the phone late in the evening and said, "I'd like to." At that point, enough time had gone by so that I said, "You'd like to what?" And she said, "Marry you." And from that moment on I never had any regrets.

I gave her a ring on August 25—my grandmother's diamond. We looked at settings at Tiffany's and so on. There was the usual announcement in *The New York Times* with Sophie's photograph. And in July of the following year we were married in Marble Collegiate Church because it was neutral religious ground: I'm Presbyterian and she's Russian Orthodox. We honeymooned in Bermuda at the Reefs, a very lovely place. I had been there before and thought Sophie would like it. We did have a very nice time.

When we came back to New York, we rented a little place on Sixtieth Street. My parents had given us a nice amount of money with which to buy some furniture, and we did straight off. Sophie was working hard and asserting herself, a real person and not a new bride pulled under by the role of being married. We were enormously happy being together. We'd have lunch together almost every day and couldn't wait to get home and see each other. I was very proud of her and of myself too, that I'd been so damned smart to latch on to her. We really felt we were the chosen pair, and this was supported by a lot of our friends. What they saw was two people who really loved each other, had become one, and yet were both still quite individualistic.

We knew where we were going, what we wanted to do, and our objectives sounded very romantic to everyone.

We had certain tastes and personality characteristics which we felt were embodied in the European way of living. It seemed very logical to begin to put together a trip to Europe, based not on sheer lark—people just weren't supposed to hop up out of two good jobs like we had and run off to Europe—but heavily business- and career-oriented. We were always caught up with a challenge of one sort or another that cemented us very strongly. That's what marriage meant to me, aside from being sexually satisfying and primitive things like that *(laughs)*. That trip was definitely one of the high points of my life. We traveled together twenty-four hours a day, never once apart for those nine months. And we developed this incredible number of affectionate little names for one another. I can remember once on that trip sitting down with her and actually writing down a list of them. It must have been twenty-five different names. Like I would call her—this is probably one of the more endearing ones—Princess Lady. She would call me Gregorabus because her former roommate was involved in Latin, and Sophie was Orabus. That one's traveled for years. Now she calls me Throck.

We made a lot of contacts on that trip and there was a great deal of play. We met some friends at Eastertime in Florence and we decided to have an Easter egg hunt. It must have been like a Fellini scene, right by the roadway as the cars are going by, and here we are, crazy people, on hands and knees crawling around in the bushes and behind statues looking for eggs.

One Sunday, when we were back in New York, Sophie was going through *The New York Times* as she faithfully did and found an ad for an architect's job. I called up and found it was the Thornton office. I thought it was remarkable that these people would advertise. It is very rare to be able to get into that office or even get an interview with them, but they wanted to see me and it was very fortunate because Roger Thornton himself was in town from California. We had a fairly lengthy talk. I explained what I had done and why I went to Europe, and he thought it was very interesting and made a lot of sense in his organization. He hired me on the spot.

Here it was again, this kind of charmed life which Sophie was beginning to call the Hobson luck. It kind of annoyed her because I wasn't out looking for a job as faithfully as I might have and right away here comes the best possible job. You see, Sophie does achieve, but she really has to work at it, whereas my success sort of comes out of the blue. I think she was jealous of me, so freely and easily moving in almost a prescribed manner. She never let me forget that she was the one who found that ad in the paper.

So I was really riding high, working as hard as I could to bring myself to the front, and at this point, Sophie is starting to soar in her career. She was in promotion at a magazine and then she was an editor there. We were associating with a pretty high level of people and enjoying that a great deal—friends from Europe, architect friends, and glamorous people in Sophie's business. She had a number of assignments that would take her down to the Islands and to Greece, and I would go along. She had lavish accommodations and endless amounts of expense money. We just wallowed in luxury. Then I was able to negotiate my own trips to Europe and we'd go simultaneously. We'd just take Paris apart and put it back together again.

Before we were married, Sophie clearly defined that she wanted to be a working woman, that she had little interest at all in children. "Children," she'd say, "I don't want them!" But I liked children and from the social connotations of marriage felt that I certainly should have a child. So there was an uneasiness about that, but I let it ride. Then Sophie just stopped using her diaphragm. She said she couldn't stand the goddamned thing anymore and she didn't care what happened. I didn't think much about it. Some time passed and all of a sudden she became enormously ill with an ill-defined disease—she was pregnant! *(laughs)*.

I liked the idea. I wanted a child to share some of my experiences, and obviously a boy would be nice. Sophie worked up until two weeks before she had Billy and approximately ten days later she was back at work. We used to talk about how it was reminiscent of the Russian peasant ladies of her ancestry having a baby in the field and bringing in the harvest that afternoon. I had this prevailing feeling that here was a remarkable woman. I mean, most women, most mothers, haven't done a damned thing in their life and here was this lady having a child really as a *part* of the rest of her life.

I had trepidations, though, about what effects it was going to have on the child, and Sophie did too. She did a lot of reading and found all kinds of psychological background to support the idea that if she was fulfilled, the child would be. This was just going to be another chapter of our successful life and right from the start Billy was a very beautiful child. We got caught up in the idea of Hobson luck again. Here we were, still sailing high in our own careers, and now we had this extraordinary child. We hired Mrs. Greely, a wonderful nurse, and though obviously we did carry our work around with us, we made a conscious effort to be at home and be with Billy, to enjoy one another as a family. It worked very well.

But there came a point in Sophie's life when she questioned the moral value of what she was doing, questioned liking fashion and clothes and the rest of her life. She didn't like to go to cocktail parties anymore, which I did. She would shoot me down constantly; she'd say if you can't talk about facts, don't talk at all, which embroiled me because I enjoy expressing myself. She had leaned heavily on my aesthetic sense and so I had selected the furniture—Eames chairs, Breuer this and that, kind of steely, hard-edged stuff—and she would say it lacked warmth and that the coldness is reflected in my personality. Sophie is very prone to finding a metaphor and using that as a personality indicator. She didn't want to accept the fact that fashion and clothing and the luxuries she had chosen to surround herself with were of importance to her. The fact was, she almost wallowed in them. I mean, she would reject them on the one hand, but loved clothes and jewelry as much as any woman I know on the other. She would say that fashion was not meaningful, that my work was uninteresting, I was uninteresting, and who wanted to be around an architect? I really got wrung out by her.

Our sex life reached a low ebb then. Sophie had virtually no interest. She could just shut things off and say, "I don't want to," which can be fine for a while, but I definitely wanted to proceed onward. It was very frustrating, but I certainly didn't think she was going to be pursuing it out-of-doors.

And then all of a sudden Sophie said she wanted to paint and quit her job. I honestly could not come up with any logical understanding of why someone who was doing so well would be so dissatisfied. But I was kind of desperate and if this was going to make her happy, even if it was a whim, I'd go along with it. So I agreed we ought to do something to change our life-style, either build a place on our land in Connecticut or buy a loft downtown so that we would have an uptown and a downtown house. I mean, I didn't have any great need to have a loft, but it sounded kind of fun, lots of space for our respective activities, and that was the scheme we finally settled on.

Sophie was enormously happy down there. It was sunny and airy. She would free-lance material in an office we set up and she would paint once in a while. She was wonderfully good at it right from the start and I was very proud of her.

SEVEN PERFECT MARRIAGES THAT FAILED

And we did have great times down there. We'd eat and entertain. We were very caught up in art collecting and we'd have painters and sculptors and photographers over. That was probably the most glamorous part of our life. We would sleep downtown some nights and uptown others.

But I started to get some inklings of something being wrong. Suspicions, almost paranoid suspicions at times. We had a party at our uptown place one evening to which we invited a fellow that I had been in the same club with at school. He was a painter, very much the loner and a very strange guy. I found him, at a distance, interesting. There were a lot of people and we were all sitting around and drinking, really getting higher than kites. And through my blurred vision, I saw Sophie and Tom talking and having a nice time with one another. Then I saw them go out in the kitchen. Some time passed. I walked into the kitchen and found them kissing. It knocked me completely out, but I didn't get angry. I kind of understood, well, they'd been drinking and that might happen. The next morning we discussed it and she said it was nothing, so I just let it pass.

Then Sophie started making it very evident that coming uptown was difficult, that she didn't like to be there, which made me kind of angry. I didn't think that was fair. Then she made it very clear that downtown was her territory and that I was coming to her place. She was very much into privacy at that point. She started staying down there at night because she wanted to get up early and start working. I thought maybe it was better to let her stay down there and live out this thing. But I was lonely, so I'd call her. Then I'd call and she wouldn't be there. The next day she'd say she had been out drawing or whatever, and one time she said she had been in jail because she had been to a meeting at NYU and they had thrown everyone in jail.

She seemed very depressed, confused, and upset. One night I called and there was no answer and I thought, "Christ, she's killed herself at the loft." So I dragged Billy

out of bed, got the car out of the garage, and went downtown, and there was no Mommy. I had to make some excuse
for Mommy not being there. It upset me enormously. She
called the next day and said she'd stayed over at her girl
friend Sally's house.

Then I went off to Europe on a business trip, and I met
this lady in Paris through friends of ours. An enormously
attractive model from South Africa, very wealthy, very sexually oriented. It was such in incredible turn-on and it was
under enormously romantic auspices. We were staying at a
little garret apartment. She knew Paris like the back of her
hand. We spent enormous sums of money, rode around in a
Rolls, and ate in extraordinary restaurants, one after the
other, two or three a night. She was very screwed up. Her
husband was Dutch and had certain cold male Dutch characteristics which she felt were just impossible. So there was
this great mutual exchange. And sex wasn't dirty, I wasn't
crude, she was enormously turned on by me. She did not
make any sense in my life if I really wanted to be practical,
but I loved her for that moment and we parted with great
sorrow and tears.

When I got back, Sophie and I went to see a psychiatrist, Dr. Meyer, and we talked about whether we should
logically separate. We talked about Sophie being downtown and me being uptown and Sophie not saying what she
was doing. Meyer is a real son of a bitch. He really aggres-
sively pursued her. We really got on her and I was saying
that I thought she was sexually incapable and I didn't think
she was capable with anyone. She said she didn't think she
was incapable and then she said, "I'm having an affair." It
all came out that she had been having an affair with Tom
for quite some time, actually close to two years. It knocked
me off my feet so much that I said, "Okay, that's it. Let's
split."

On the way home—she was going to stay downtown and
I was to go uptown—we went into a bar and got a beer. I

could have killed her at that point. I mean, the anger was really finally coming. "Fine," I said, "you'll never see Billy again." She wanted Billy to come and live with her and her lover. And I said, "I'm suing you for divorce and I'm going to sue for the custody of Billy." And she said, "If that's the way it's got to be, I'll give up Bill. I can't, but I will."

She's telling me she found a way of life that she likes. He's very poor, but she likes this. Bohemian—she's really into that. I really hated him. I concocted this huge fantasy about what I ought to be doing in this situation. Definitely, one choice was to call a lawyer, second was to go down and confront this guy and kill him. So I talked with my lawyer, who convinced me that a hard-line approach might work, that I should see how long Sophie would last down there. Because to everyone concerned, except Sophie, what she was doing was so absolutely ridiculous. I thought she would come back and we could negotiate something. I'd had an affair, she'd had an affair, we're over with this kind of moral crap, and let's address what we can have, have always had, together.

So I waited. I got inklings that she was enormously unhappy. This man Tom was totally inflexible. She was living in a place where she couldn't even take a bath. Very quickly she wanted to try and make a go of it with me again. We kind of outlined what we wanted to do and embarked again, both of us seeing our respective doctors. But it never really worked again. We were very disappointed and unhappy. We tried it for a year and then we just floated right out of the marriage. She got another loft with Billy, and I stayed uptown.

Looking back, I can see that there were a number of goals Sophie and I began to explore together, and from a selfish point of view, they represented an enrichment of myself. And Sophie assimilated part of my life too, like she acquired an enormous amount of taste from me. Maybe we were operating on a very high level, doing good things, but we were not really moving, not growing the way I like to. I think I was depressed for a very long time without knowing it. I am really very sorry, more than that, enormously unhappy, that we didn't work it out, but I can say this too: As soon as I separated, there was an enormous burst of energy. I learned to branch out and explore. I learned something important literally the day we separated—that you can find other people with those basic ingredients. I've never felt such joy at being alive. Just because things with Sophie couldn't work out, the world is not this strange, tortured place. There can be other people you can be happy with.

JENNIFER AND DAVID
Chronology

1961	First meet at Lenox summer school of music and art.
1964	Meet again in Lenox.
1965	Wedding.
1965–66	Living in New York loft.
1967–1970	David teaching at Kansas State; Jennifer weaving, photographing.
1968	Involvement with Cindy, Maria, others.
1970–74	Back to New York, working.
1971	Guatemala.
1973	Jennifer's operation.
1974	Involvement with Charlotte.
August, 1974	Jennifer's trip to Maine.
September, 1974	They separate.

3

The
Super Erotics

For people who feel sexually unfulfilled in marriage, no myth is more tantalizing than that of the Super Erotics—a rare union of two sensual people who are a perfect sexual match. Overwhelmingly attracted to one another, they are constantly breaking new sexual barriers, leading each other to new erotic highs. Their relationship is dramatic and intense, overflowing with the passion that links them together. If men's and women's most basic desire is sexual fulfillment, then surely their marriage must be the ideal.

Jennifer and David Schneider were drawn to one another from the start by the dream of a passionate life.

Slim, blond-haired, and bright-eyed, Jennifer combines an apple-pie freshness with a seductive, smoky sexiness. She acts out her stories with dramatic gestures, sudden confidential whispers, and a throaty laugh. She is a professional photographer who recently completed a photo essay on Africa.

JENNIFER:
Dave was a student at the Lenox summer school of music and art, and I was the maid. It was this huge estate,

35

grander than the White House. Washington slept there. My job was to make punch for parties, clean the studios, make beds, whatever. I was a small-town Massachusetts girl, with no idea of the outside world except through books. And he was a very crazy fellow.

The first time I became aware of Dave, he was doing little watercolors behind the barn, and I thought they were really beautiful. I remember talking to him about that. He seemed so stable—and so crazy. I remember one thing that summer—there was a party and all of the artists were there dancing. And someone came running up to the party and said, "Schneider is up in the painting studio—and he's taking off all his clothes!" And I thought, Wow! That's one of the most far-out things that's ever happened in this town! *(laughs)*. And then he proceeded to literally roll down the driveway! It was harmless and beautiful and just set everybody on their ear. He's known for that—out of the blue, he would do something completely wackadoo.

I was a real rebel. I used to date the town criminal. Whenever he wasn't in reform school, I was running off to Pittsfield with him in a stolen truck. I think I always just wanted to get out. And I had really no power to do it except through those rebellious kind of things. Or sex. Fucking at fourteen. One of the reasons I did it was because I was horny. And the other reason was that there was nothing else to do! There was no other way to connect with another person. I certainly was not a good girl—and that was very important there. I'm doing the same thing now, but it's OK. I don't care what people think anymore, but I cared then.

Dave and I were very friendly, and at the end of that summer, my mother and I drove him to the train station—he was wearing a corduroy suit—and I didn't see him again for three years. I'd come home from New York for a couple of days and I went to this lake—Gabby Pond—and as I was sitting on the beach here's this bearded fellow and he saw me at the same moment. We pointed at each other and said, "I know you." He said, "I don't really remember your name." And I remember saying, "Little Mary Sunshine." We talked, we walked, we swam, we made love in a gazebo. We spent twenty-four hours together. Everything was magical that night. The light was silver. And it just felt like my soul had been touched by the sight of this man. I really just felt literally swept by him. I just surrendered myself. Take me! *(laughs)*.

The next day we came back to the city with his friends Milt and Sally. In the back seat Dave and I just couldn't keep our hands off of each other. And from that time on, we stayed together. I had an apartment on Sixty-fifth and First, a studio with a tiny kitchen and a knockout shower which we loved. He was renting a studio on Thirteenth Street with a bed that is narrower than a couch. That summer broke all records for heat. We were glued together on that tiny cot. I don't know how we did it, but it was just the flush of it all. I'd been attracted to men before, but there had never been anything like this. I felt on top of the world. It was just so great to have such a good time with somebody and there weren't all these heavy regulations. He just seemed to really enjoy me. And I really enjoyed him. One night he came to stay with me and he brought me a copy of *Catch-22* and a tube of vaginal foam. *Catch-22* and vaginal foam! I thought he was so incredibly imaginative. And we stayed up all night reading *Catch-22* to each other and laughing ourselves silly.

Our whole relationship was incredibly sexual. We used to fuck on stairs and under waterfalls—all over the place. Dave was someone I could really share with. Before I met Dave I slept around a lot, but after I'd been with him for a year I had eyes for not another soul. No one could be as good. And I thought, I've done all this wild shit and here's a man I really love that really cares about me, and yes, I was ready to settle down. My parents really wanted me to get married too—they wouldn't let us sleep together in their house! So we were driving to the lake, and we'd gotten just about to the country club on top of the hill, and just before going down the hill, he asked me to marry him! *(laughs)*. "What?" I said. "Do my ears mislead me?" And then I said, "*Yes!*"

I wasn't pursuing a career then. I thought what I needed was a man, one man who was pursuing his own goal, and I would throw myself behind it. I always felt Dave was a great artist. I felt I was expected to go to college, get married, and have a kid and two cars or two kids and a car. I was supposed to be somebody's smart wife.

My parents were ecstatic! His parents—no good! I wasn't Jewish. And I had these medical problems—tumors on the cervix. They offered him money to leave me, and he was hysterical. Back and forth from me to his family, from his family to me. He wanted us to just pick up and go somewhere and I said, We can't do that—you need them. In a month, maybe six months or a year or something, you're gonna hate me for taking you away from your family. So I went to Dave's mom and I said, "Look—I really love your son. I really want to be his wife. I want you to go to my gynecologist with me and I want him to explain to you exactly what's going on in my body so that you don't have any wrong ideas about what's taking place." So I took her to my doctor and introduced her as "my mother-in-law-to-be" and told him to tell her the straight stuff. He was terrific. He said now I was fine.

Came time for the wedding and we were all there. My father gave me away and his mother and father gave him away! Which flipped me out. But it was an incredibly romantic wedding, under the hemlock in my parents' yard. Raoul, Dave's best man, had traded in an air conditioner for my wedding dress. The father of one of my best friends from school was justice of the peace, and he married us. No religion at this wedding. There were vows, but they were very personal—it had to do with *us* sanctioning *us*.

My dad has films of Dave the morning before the wedding, wandering around the backyard carrying bouquets of
flowers and looking incredibly handsome, like something
out of *Elvira Madigan*. Dave built an arbor and my mom
got hanging fuchsias and roses. I went out and picked wild
flowers and took them to this lady in Stockbridge who put
them all together so all the women in the party had wild-
flower bouquets. During the ceremony—this I'll never forget as long as I live—there were eleven women from both
our families, all standing in a row, all made up beautifully,
and all crying!

My mom made the wedding cake in the shape of a bride.
It was chocolate, our favorite, with white-chocolate icing.
And I made the first cut in the crotch! *(laughs)*. After the
ceremony we all went to the lake and got drunk on champagne and danced. To this day everyone says it was the most
fun they ever had at a wedding.

After our honeymoon, we went back to New York to
Dave's loft. I taught in the Headstart program three hours a
day. We went to dinners and invited people over for dinner
a lot. We didn't have much money, but we sure had good
times, just being with our friends and talking about art.
Dave decorated the loft. It was very chaotic and fanciful, a
playground, really. If we ever had a bad time, all we had to
do was go off in a corner and fuck and everything was
wonderful.

That summer I was sick every day. My body felt different. And I thought, "Holy Moly. I'm pregnant." Dave was
so happy. We called our parents and everything. Dave had
gotten a teaching job at Kansas State and somewhere on the
way there I started to bloat and felt so funny. I probably
picked the worst physician in the entire Midwest. I started
hemorrhaging in his office and he was so cruel and callous. I
came screaming out of there and Dave was aghast. Whether

I'd been pregnant or not, I wasn't now. I was just heartbroken and Dave was very loving. There was that awful feeling of what can you do except care.

So that's how things started at Kansas State. There I was having lost that baby. Miserable. But Dave came to the rescue by suggesting I take a weaving course. I did and I really enjoyed it. I started to like some people. We got involved in university life and everybody liked Dave—everybody always likes him. We ate a lot and we fucked a lot and we laughed a lot.

There was a lot of purity in Dave's feeling, you know. But I started to see that he was very unchecked. He was not a controlled thing. Dave's first outburst toward me was the night that I developed my first roll of film. I had gone out to a farm somewhere and taken some pictures and I was just dying to see what they looked like. We went to a movie with our friends Sarah and Jim, who had a darkroom, and afterward I cornered Jim and I said, "Can I come over and develop my film?" He said, "Sure," so I did.

Sarah and Dave were upstairs having a drink together, and Jim and I were in this little basement darkroom developing the film, and I thought it was fantastic. We were washing the film when Sarah came downstairs and said, "There's something wrong with Dave." We go upstairs and he's sitting in the corner in a chair, drinking. And the whole atmosphere of the evening just became so tense, so heavy.

We drove back across town to our apartment and I couldn't figure it out. It was the first time I really felt closed out. He turned around and started screaming about what a crappy housekeeper I was and— Oh, man, I don't even remember it all. But his words hit me like wham, bang, boom, wrock. So I said, "Well, I don't know what's the matter with you, and I don't know where all of this is coming from, but I'm going to take a walk. When you return to being a human being, maybe I'll come back."

I sat down by the river and I just cried and cried, wondering what was going on. Working with my film was an incredible high, and then this incredible down. I mean, I wasn't the world's best housekeeper, but—

I went back to the apartment and there he was, crying, upset. And he said, "I'll cut off my hands before I'll do that again to you, you know." I said, "Don't cut off your hands. Tell me what happened." And he said, "I don't know. I was upset." I never got an answer to that. I think it was all about possessiveness and my wanting to be in the darkroom with Jim. He was jealous, which really kind of disturbed me because I had never even considered any other man. It had never occurred to me. And now it occurred to me, you know. So anyway, after all this confusion and crying, we made love, which always seemed to be the way to seal these things up again, and that was it.

I had this friend, Cindy. I felt very akin to her, and Dave enjoyed her too. Then I started sensing some sexual vibes between them. One night the three of us went to the movies, and I never was more uncomfortable in my life. I knew something was coming and I knew I wasn't going to like it. On the way to the movies, we were laughing it up, but the laughter was a little too high-pitched. And in the movie I knew that his left hand was on her and his right hand was on me. I didn't know what to say or do and I really trusted Cindy, you know. So we all left the movie, sort of snuggling up, and we went to her house. Dave undressed us and we all ended up in bed. No, I never said no. I mean I really like sex, any kind of sex. But I was upset because it was sort of their way of getting it on with my approval. Dave kept saying that since Cindy was my best friend we would all really enjoy it. But it was really his trip and he's the one who fucked us both over. He saw her again, and I knew it, and I was terribly hurt. We never talked about it, but I wanted to get back at him. Yeah. That's when I started looking at men. And I also started looking at women.

That summer we went canoeing a lot on the Tuttle Creek. Dave and his friend Joe built the canoe. It was beautiful. I had Joe's wife Andrea to talk to, and·she was very perceptive. We discussed the hypothetical situation of sex with another woman. What do you think about that, Andrea? She saw its possibilities *(laughs)* and found it very titillating that I brought up the subject. I really didn't know anything about it.

That November we put on *Marat/Sade*. I played the wife of the director of the institution and Dave—try this one on—played De Sade. He loved his role, and he was really good! He even changed one of his speeches one night—there was some drunken asshole in the audience making noise— without changing character, completely within the limits of the play, he addressed that guy and made him shut up! I mean, he was really in control.

In the play, my role really was one of response to De Sade, and I started to see how that *really* matched our marriage. One night after rehearsal we were having a nosh or something, and one of the young girls in the cast came up to us. I was not liking Dave that night at all; he was very De Sade and I was very Madame Coumier. In this squeaky voice the girl said, "Oooh, Mrs. Schneider—you're such a cuuuute couple." I couldn't think of a worse thing anybody could have said then. We were not cute!

I met Charles in rehearsals, and he reminded me of one of my first lovers. I wanted an affair. I wanted to try it out. Charles and I—just a few times. In his office. In the theater. Yeah, I enjoyed that. Of course, Dave never knew. God, no! That's not my style! I don't think it's any of his business, really. But he always made his affairs my business. For which I didn't appreciate him at all. Charles—there was nothing to it emotionally. I enjoyed him. He's a nice guy.

One of the biggest things that Dave loved me for was my spontaneity, my out-of-the-blue wanting to go off and do something whatever it might be without regard for what it's going to cost or how long it's going to take. I mean, if I think of something and I want to do it, I'll just do it. And the rest be damned.

And then I fell in love with a woman. Bananas. And it really turned me around. She comes out of a very foreign, European background. She's very intelligent, incredibly sensitive, very talented. From a whole other space.

Maria and I met at a party. It wasn't like we hadn't seen each other before, this lady and I. But this time it was magic drawing us to each other. We were just drunk with it. We couldn't keep our eyes off each other. I mean, never could I have dreamed, but there it was. She and I had this incredible kiss, right there in front of the whole world! It happened in spite of everything I knew, had been taught, had experienced. There it came, as pure as the driven snow.

Maria had never had an affair with a woman before either. We both had sort of the same impetuousness—sexually, anyway. We had some marvelous scenes together, with other men too. It was always dynamite with the two of us. And there was tenderness too. We could be each other's mothers; we could be each other's children; we could be each other's sisters, husbands, wives.

Her husband used to go out of town a lot and we used to get together at her house. I used to spend nights there. I was terrible to Dave, and I used to feel real guilty about it. The three of us got it on together one time—more than one time, actually. I wasn't crazy about it. It was better than with Cindy, yes, because it was my movie. But it wasn't really what I had in mind.

Maria and I used to go all over the place. And we were alone constantly. We used to even go to a motel just to be alone. There was always this intrigue, not being seen together. And it was torment to Dave. I was constantly trying to make him feel that I really did care about him, but I was always running off to her. I really did care about him.

But someone would have had to lock me up to keep me from going to her.

A lot of tension built up. I felt I was over my head because of having so many feelings—for her, for him, for the marriage, for what are people going to say, for what am I sexually. Dave used to go crazy, screaming about how I was a disgrace. He's a European male, you know, brought up in a very old-fashioned, traditional way, and he found it repulsive! But he never really said anything, except was I going to leave him? And I said no. I really wanted him too, you see. I loved him and it was my marriage. It's funny, Maria and Dave were similar in many ways. They both are very witty, they both are observers. They both had a lustiness that's delightful. And they're both very manipulative.

So here are these two people, revolving around me, involved with each other because of me, and I felt powerless. The love affair ended because I felt the only other alternative was suicide. I couldn't bear being so torn, and being made responsible, not only for him but for her. I'm not responsible for either of them, am I?

I didn't really see where to go next. I met a psychologist at that time and I seduced him so I could pick his brain. I really needed help. He also needed help. He was having a very hard time getting it up. So I got him up and he got me on *(laughs)*. I really did benefit from his advice, and I added a little spark to his otherwise very boring life.

When I finally ended my relationship with Maria, it was very painful for both of us. But it really had to end and there was no good way to do it. It just hurt, and I felt terribly guilty for all the torment I know I caused both of them.

All this time Dave used to throw it at me about not having a kid. I used to go through all this testing and stuff to find a way to make it possible. It was hell. And then if he was pissed off at me, invariably I'd hear about how we couldn't have a kid because of me. I felt I was in danger of losing him because I couldn't conceive a child.

I made an appointment with my doctor to talk about what's going on here, and we went to see him after his office hours. He explained that one of my ovaries collapsed and my uterus can't hang on to a fertilized egg. Now Dave has the kind of energy that could turn a crowd around. Well, that kind of energy can be used all kinds of ways. It can be wonderfully creative. Or it can be so hostile that you'd rather die than be in its presence—and that's what he was like the day we went to see the doctor. Horrible! He couldn't even answer the simplest questions. Like how he felt about adoption.

When we got out of there I said, "You are the meanest motherfucker alive. How could you do that? This doctor extended his hand because he's known me for so many years and he really likes me. You're so hot to have a kid, but when we go and try to find some way to deal with it, you won't even answer the most civil of questions. Where's your head at? What kind of kid do you want? Do you want a kid? What is this?"

He finally said, "Maybe I don't really want kids. Maybe I want a kid because I think I'm supposed to have one." It was just another way of not dealing with things. There was no way I could win.

Finally I said, "Look—I never, ever, ever, want to hear about a child again! It will not be discussed! I will never bring it up!" And I never did. That was the end of the baby.

Through all this—we were back in New York by this time—when we were together, we put on a good show: Mr. and Mrs. Married. Oh yeah, we were terrific. Dressed nice, always seen together. We were a good host and hostess and we were affectionate to each other. There was a tremendous amount of pleasure and when it was there it was like nothing had ever happened.

In 1971 we spent three glorious weeks in Guatemala, and we both considered that our real honeymoon. We stayed in a place surrounded by mountains where it was like the eternal spring the poets write about. Everything felt so perfect. The thought of leaving brought great pain. I really felt that we had found Paradise. And why are we leaving again? There's someplace to go from Paradise? New York, you say?

Back at home we got along fine for a while. I was working twelve, sixteen hours a day, really slaving away at photography to make up for lost time. And Dave was working toward an exhibit of his work. Then, here again, the old cancer reappeared. It was October of 1973 when I received the news that I had something really serious to deal with. They wanted to rush me into surgery. A vulvectomy. Hold on there, man, we've got two arms, we've got two legs, two eyes, two ears— Got one cunt! I wasn't going to let anybody rush me into anything. I really wasn't convinced that living without a cunt and without cancer—for who knows how long—was really the solution for my life. I wrote a letter to my surgeon and I asked a zillion questions. Was it dangerous? What was going to happen afterward? What was it going to be like walking and pissing and fucking? I felt much better after I'd gotten the letter off. Our sex was great that night and part of the reason was that I thought it might be the last I'd ever have.

Dave was getting very hyper too now. He was getting almost no sleep, working day and night on his sculpture. Most of the time he was flying his own wings, not lending me any emotional support. I understood the high, working all the time—but I also felt that he had deserted me. If he had been looking for a way to have revenge, I felt that he had found it and that it was really cruel. I never forgave him.

And then the gods decided to play their hands for me. There was a convention of the Honch Gynecologists of America or something. And during that convention, the policy was changed to treating my condition as a local problem by removing whatever was the damaged, diseased area and leaving the rest of it alone. I was saved.

Okay, now I guess it's time for the story of the ménage that worked *(laughs)*. We met this incredibly beautiful woman, Charlotte, really lush, oozing it, who's very heavily involved in the whole S-M scene. She used to do things like tickle guys' balls with a whip and stuff. No hurting, no nasty stuff, but she was heavy into it. She used to take pictures of people fist fucking. Gosh, fist fucking. Since the De Sade adventure Dave decided that he really liked that whole S-M thing. His drawings started to be very explicitly sexual— beautiful sexual ladies wrapped in rosy satin in very suggestive positions. And we became somehow involved with Charlotte.

When we all hopped in the sack it was really good, he was very loving. I was happy that he had someone else to fuck because I really dug Charlotte and I didn't feel threatened by her in any way. I saw what it might do for him and consequently for us. I knew that he'd go to her house and that didn't bother me at all, because I thought she would probably teach him a few things. And I thought, Man, he couldn't have a more dynamite teacher. If anyone was going to show him a few things, it would be her. I thought it was beautiful, but he was very guilty about it. And I think that he didn't like it so much that it didn't bother me. But for me, sex just isn't exclusive. I really feel about sex the way I feel about food: I don't like eating the same thing every day even if it is my favorite. I want to be able to sleep with whoever I want without guilt, without labels, without anything.

But for Dave there was always the guilt. He had his three or four affairs and I always had to hear about every one of them. Like the time Dave went to New Hampshire and had an affair with a virgin. He's lucky his parents didn't hear about it. He called to tell me about her because he was sure that someone else would. And he wanted to be the first one to tell me. Swell call. "Thanks a million."

So it was either throwing it in my face, or these ugly deceptions. Like this one day, a Sunday, he mumbled something about how we were going to have this nice day together. But when I wake up in the morning, he's out of bed, dressed, and says he has to go out for a little while. Three hours later, he comes back, right? And I see right away that I've just been handed a laid man! I said, "You really disgust me with your lies. Why do you always lie to me?" He didn't really want to be secretive or he would have been cool about it and I wouldn't have been aggravated. He wanted to do me in and he did. I was so pissed off that I could hardly see straight. He came back just in time so that we could go to his folks' for lunch. Real cushy. From this lady, pick up the wife and go to Mama's!

That afternoon, I went to a photo exhibit on Staten Island and he insisted on tagging along. He ruined my day. And later that night when we got home I said, "Look, this is terrible. I'm going to leave for a few days."

I stayed at a friend's studio and I was miserable! Every day he called and we would talk on the phone and cry and he would beg me to come home. And I'd say to him, "To what? Why? How are we going to do this?" And he'd say, "Just come home. Just come home." After the fourth or fifth day we met for lunch, but I didn't see that there was any progress. I started saying, "There's been something very seriously wrong for years. You thrive on feeling shitty. You refuse my assistance, and that affects me terribly. You go from being morose to coming home with flowers and I never know which end is up. Is your whole life fantasy? You come to the edge of action and you always opt to slam the door and bolt it. I can't live with that."

Finally I suggested we go to a psychiatrist, a third party of his choice. And he said, "I don't want to hear about this anymore. I don't want to discuss it." So, the only thing on my mind was to get out of there. I wanted to go up to Maine, where I could feel at peace with myself and my surroundings, and leave him as quickly as possible.

That month away was one long, marvelous high. Being with this wonderful man I met, being alone, being with friends. Feeling so good—no anxieties, no frustrations, just taking life as it comes. Nothing was agonizing or painful or upsetting. There were many situations like hitching out of St. Andrews with Michael, and stopping to take pictures along the way—where if I'd been with Dave, he would have been saying things like, "It's raining. What if we don't get a ride? When's the ferry going to come in?" I didn't know the answers to any of those questions. I just wait and hit it.

When I came back to New York I went home and there was nobody there. I went in the shower and Dave came home and he looked beautiful. It was kind of quiet and smiles. I was glad to see him. And then, after chatting for a while, I said, "You know, I don't think we should live together anymore. It just hasn't worked, and there seems to be too much that neither of us is able to deal with. I met someone and it's not because of him that I don't want to live with you, but it's because of how I was able to be with him. I was just able to be me. That's all."

I tried to explain myself to him as best I understood myself so that he wouldn't feel that it was just him. And I really did give it my all for a long, long time. But my nature combined with his and the unbendingness of the two together just didn't make it.

"You don't have to do those dances anymore," I said. And I said good-bye.

David Schneider is charged with energy. A powerfully built man with a wild red beard and sparkling eyes, he is a natural actor who lives out his stories with obvious relish. He holds a master of fine arts degree from a prestigious

*university and at thirty-five is an accomplished artist whose
surreal, sensual wood sculptures have been exhibited at
universities and in New York galleries. He still lives in the
loft-studio where he and Jennifer lived for the last five years
of their marriage.*

DAVID:

From the start I saw that Jennifer was very different
from any other woman I had known, and different from me
too. She had all those things I admired and wanted—she was
independent, swinging, sexual, adventurous, enthusiastic. I
tended to be morose and serious and thought you had to
work at life. And it seemed to me that Jenny was just in it, in
life. Of course, I've learned since that she just did a different
kind of working-at-life than I did.

I was at a music and art summer school up in her
hometown when we first met. The whole thing was just so
romantic and so gorgeous. I was up in the country doing the
things that I really love to do, painting and drawing and
talking about art and being with people who love art. You
see, I was born in Russia and grew up all over Europe where
everybody was the enemy, and then in 1950 my parents
came to New York by some kind of fluky thing. So Lenox
must have been tied up with an idea of really being in an
American place. There was some kind of peacefulness and
ease and coolness about it. I was just a pushover for it. I
always loved Lenox and whenever I had a chance I would go
back and visit my old teachers and be in that magical place
again.

One weekend I went up with some friends and we went
to Gabby Pond, and—boom!—there was Jenny. It had been
three years and she did not even live there anymore—she
was just up for the weekend. It was really sort of A Beautiful
Story.

We had a drink and talked and that night, out in the

landscape, we made love. It was just terrific. I felt, here was someone who really, really wanted to ball, who really enjoyed it and really looked forward to it. It was totally different from any other experience I'd had before—more open, more joyful, much more guilt-free. And it was so very erotic. It wasn't something that you finally win your way to, or convince your way to, or overcome difficulties and finally get to. It was just— Oh, good! Pull your pants down! Let's do it now!

After that night, we went back to New York together. We liked each other, we liked being together, and we really enjoyed making love. Jenny was very sensual. We used to love to bathe together, shower together. Jenny had an air conditioner in her place, and I remember it used to blow on us when we made love.

I was sort of being bohemian then. As well as learning about art, I was learning about being an artist. You put on various masks, you know, and do those things that it seems like artists should do. You visit teachers and their friends and meet other artists and sort of learn the life-style. I think one of the things Jenny wanted in New York was a life-style like that. She quit her night job at an ice cream parlor and started working as an artist's model. We were living a very romantic life, young artist and model.

Jenny had run away from home when she was a kid, and there were always those rebellious, gypsyish moves in her. She needed somebody to take care of her, and I needed somebody to take care of. At that time there wasn't that strong consciousness that women have given us about those things now. I mean, I approve of that new thinking—I just wish they'd hurry up and do it so we could all relax! (laughs).

But then everything was so right for us, so easy for us, and the passion was so overwhelming that we fell in love. One weekend we were up in Lenox again and we went to all the places we'd gone to that summer that we remet and on the road to Gabby Pond I said, "Hey, Jenny, look, why don't we get married?" I hadn't planned it. I was just in the car and it was beautiful and, Let's make it forever!

Things got a little rough then. My folks didn't like the idea of my marrying someone with a health condition, and they made some pretty extreme offers to show me exactly how they felt. It's the Eastern European personality, you know—the mystery of disease. Of course, it was the wrong thing to do for what they desired. It just set me even stronger into doing what I wanted to do. After the wedding plans were made, Jenny's mother once said to me, "You *are* going ahead and marrying Jenny, aren't you?"

"Of course," I said. "God, I love her."

We got married up in Lenox. We hired a string quartet from Tanglewood. There was lots of food and drink and good feeling. Jenny was radiant and gorgeous. Oh, God! It was not just a meaningless piece of paper for us. It was a ceremony that achieved some psychic union. There was that whole primitive element in it. We talked later about how it was different being married and having had that rite—that our relationship was solider, somehow fuller, there was more in it now. I still believe that the life two married people have together is richer, and has more rewards.

We had been given a car for the honeymoon, and Jenny drove all the time. Driving was totally alien to me, so it always seemed easier to depend on Jenny to drive wherever we were going. And she just loved to go anywhere. We went down more roads with "Do Not Enter" signs in the Maine woods. At the end we'd wave and say, "Hi, folks. We took a wrong turn and could we please turn around in your front yard?" And we'd drive back, laughing all the time.

We got lost at sea on our honeymoon, in one of those little plywood punt things off Swan's Island. There was a fog and we couldn't see anything and the water kept coming back and coming back. All I knew was that I had to keep rowing. I rowed for about four or five hours without stopping, just watching for signs. Meanwhile, Jenny was fishing! *(laughs)*. She was really worried, right? What a joke! It's a goddamn farce, let me tell you. I've been saying lately that there are more banana peels out here than I was led to believe.

So there we were, Just Married and in tiptop shape. Money, lots of money from the wedding. Dreams of exhibiting and becoming a famous artist. And kids, we're going to have kids. A place in the country. Those first years in New York were very happy.

Before I go on, I should tell you this: Jenny was the first girl I had met who really loved to ball and I really got into that. I love women and I've always loved women. And I think that being married freed me from an insecurity that I had had before. Now I found that I could be open and loving and charming and flirting in a very open way, and that women responded, and that I enjoyed it.

When we got to Kansas State Jenny had a miscarriage, so right away we were trying to make her pregnant again. There was something about taking her temperature to gauge when she was ovulating, so there was that little bit of mechanics involved in it that made it a really conscious act. You know, like we've really got to ball tonight because tonight's the right night. And there was the recommendation that we have sex approximately every four days so that the sperm count could grow or something like that. All that machinery made it very difficult. And ... goddamn it, it's too interesting not to tell. I mean, I might as well tell it all, right?

Cindy had been a friend of Jenny's and mine for a while. And one night the three of us went to see that movie, *Barbarella*. It was very sensual, and I found myself in the grips of this fantasy of making love to both of them—and all three of us making love together, which to me, at that time, was a far-out place. But I knew that it could happen, I knew it in my bones. *Barbarella* was a real turn-on. It had just the right elements, the eroticism and the kind of dreaminess to do things like this. We went back to Cindy's house and we made it to bed, together, all three of us. I was completely out of my mind. It was an erotic peak like I had never, never reached before. There they were, both of them, on the bed with their dresses up. I mean, two beautiful cunts, you know. It was gorgeous, just gorgeous.

The next thing is so funny, so funny and terrible, it really is. I'm really enthralled by Cindy's body—she's very tall, thin, angular, and I'm really enthralled by the possibility of this new sexual union. But at the same time I have a very clear sense of my allegiance to Jenny; I have some fucked-up sense of being polite, of totally ridiculous priorities. Who teaches us protocol in these situations? *(laughs)*. I'll tell you. Rule Number One for a married couple balling a stranger is that the first orgasm belongs to the wife. I just worried it to death, but I didn't do the right thing. The first orgasm was Cindy's, and in the throes of it Jenny said something like, "That belongs to me. . . . " It was terrible, but funny too. Immediate panic and guilt and fear on my part resulted in an instant "soft-on"! So Cindy went into the next room and checked her daughter and finally lay down, kind of dozed off. I'm taking care of Jenny and placating her and finally we do make love.

The next morning was OK. We were friendly, but it was like, That was it. We're not going to do this again. Jenny and I talked about it and it was, Yes, Jenny. I love you and I like Cindy, but there's nothing between us. That's the end of it.

Then one day, Cindy and I and a friend, Andy Morrison, were all out on the lawn in front of the school and Andy was massaging Cindy. She was lying on the ground and he was kneeling in front of her and massaging her shoulders and it was a very sexual gesture. We were both turned on by her and also turning her on. Andy had to leave and I was left with Cindy. So I went back into the studio where I was working, and Cindy was there. We were just talking and continuing in the same vein and I think we must have touched. We went down the hallway, ostensibly to get a drink of water, and went into a drawing room, where there was a mattress for the model to rest on. The school was empty, but we knew Jenny was supposed to meet me there. We just got into that room and were hugging and kissing when we heard steps in the hallway. Boom, we walk out of the room and there's Jenny. So nothing had happened, but of course, everything had happened. You understand that I'm not proud of these things.

The next thing—it really seems strange to me now—was our going to this psychiatrist out there. Jenny's attitude was, "Dave is interested in having this extramarital affair and why is this happening?" It was like I was getting my hand slapped because I never, never wanted to go to an analyst and I still don't. So that was my punishment in a way. But here is the peculiar part: We never mentioned to him that incident between the three of us. Maybe we even exchanged a look and that look said, This is something that we will not mention, right? Like there are some limits that were not to be crossed.

I'm sort of at a loss now, because the next part of this story involves Jenny much more than it involves me. This is a part of the story that had to do with a—a very strong experience for her and an incidental one for me.

Somewhere in that time out there in Kansas, there was a student in my class, an older woman—(laughs) older? She must have been thirty at the time and I was, maybe, twenty-six. She was really beautiful, exotic, charming, funny, sophisticated, wealthy, European, erudite, everything—beautiful legs, beautiful body . . . and boom! I was under her power immediately. My friend Andy called it "cunt-struck."

Maria was a very passionate woman who was having some trouble with her marriage, so we had this thing where we just balled wherever we could, in the supply room of the sculpture department and everywhere. The danger and excitement made me want more. So I was caught in the dynamo of my fantasy again, both Jen and Maria together. Two beautiful erotic women and me. I mean, just think of all those shapes, all that softness just coming together. It's aesthetics, you know. So I encourage a friendship between Jenny and Maria and they hit it off just like that. It was the Devil in me that made me do it because the Devil had his own ax to grind. Soon I was being used as well as using, but I was always two steps behind.

We were all very intense. Excitement, danger, illicit everything, wonderful everything. But while there's this stuff going on on top, there's other stuff being washed away on the bottom. We were riding this enormous high, and in the meantime there was terrible pain and destruction going on in a part of ourselves that we did not pay any attention to. We were treating what was going on like it was very casual, but it wasn't casual at all. Maria and I would ball every once in a while. But Maria and Jenny—there was magic in that union. They were both beautiful—Jenny's very blond, long blond reddish hair, and Maria's very light-skinned with black hair and eyes—both gorgeous and a real knockout together. But all the while I'm minimizing their relationship so that I could continue having my little thing with Maria and also on occasion have both of them, I'm being gnawed away by jealousy.

You have to remember that Jenny and I have always been very openly sexual and everything was in our realm of fantasy. I think these things were more my fantasy and Jenny sort of went along with it. But there must have been something in all that that was satisfying to Jen. I hope so, anyway. I'd really hate to think that she really hated all those things that we did wind up doing. I believe she sort of went along with it because it seemed so necessary for me to do it. I don't think she would have gone out and done it on her own.

Things at Kansas got worse, more intense. One night Jenny and Maria wouldn't let me in the house. They were at Maria's and I think they had taken peyote or something. Another time, the three of us went to Boston—Jenny and Maria would drive *(laughs)*—and on the way back I said, "Jenny, last night was really terrible, you got up and you went into the living room and you spent three hours with Maria and I was awake all that time. I can't take that anymore." But they can't help themselves and it's magic and it was in the stars and they're both Pisces and they have their horoscopes done together and there is just too much mystery in their relationship for them to look at it. But *I'm* fucked up about it, you see? They're terrific in it, but I'm fucked up about it.

After we moved back to New York, whatever Jenny and Maria had together sort of disappeared. And then Jenny and I were happy again. We really did a lot together, grew a lot and were more established in our desires and as people who act in the world. The happiest times we had together these last few years were talking about Jenny's photographs. She had been in shows and had sold work and it was apparent that she was very talented. We'd sit at the table and look at her photos and talk about how particular spatial themes were developing. Many happy hours. And I was drawing, trying to do something about my career. We worked together, each of us getting better, and we went to Maine to look for land and to Guatemala, and the great lovemaking was there again.

During this time, Jenny had to have another operation. I never liked thinking about her operations. It was something I was conscious of, something I knew was imminent, but it did not even cross my mind that Jenny was under this terrible cloud all this time. I should have realized that Jenny's feelings of herself as a woman and a sexual being must have been jeopardized by these various operations. I really wish I had been more aware and more intelligent about it. Just paid more attention to what I said, to what I did.

But as time went on we were both beginning to lead very different lives. I was teaching and had other jobs, so that my day was pretty much organized out of necessity. Jenny's days were a little more open most of the time, and Jenny's very fond of sleeping. She's a talented sleeper, loves to sleep and sleeps well. She also loves to stay up late *(laughs)*. Can't stand to sleep, loves to stay up and have a cigarette, another chat, another cup of coffee. Loves to sleep late in the morning, though, and since she's a very elegant person, she likes a casual rising, you know, with showering and eating, coffee, cigarette, making phone calls, feeding the cat. So her day would begin very late and end very late and when I would get home from work there wouldn't be anybody home. I didn't like that.

Also, I couldn't deal with Jenny's not making any money, and I couldn't deal with my inability to tell her that she had to go out and make some money and support her goddamned hobby. Finally, I said, "Jenny, you've got to go out and make some money."

"What do you want me to do, work at Macy's?"

"Of course I don't want you to work at Macy's." You know, Mr. Nice Guy doesn't let his wife work at Macy's. Meanwhile, I was holding down two jobs and getting more and more upset about not being able to work in my studio. Finally, I spent a week stoned, just doing drawings and smoking. I ate very little so I could stay high. I would stay up all night and draw, take a nap, get up, smoke pot, and go back to the drawings. I didn't care about the goddamned bills. I'd always felt the responsibility. And Jenny had always said, "Don't be so tense about money. It'll come from somewhere, it'll be all right. It's always been all right." But toward the end of that month when I was really working on those drawings, Jenny said, "You know, this is really not a good time for you to relax about money." And I said, "Yeah, I know. That's right. I guess I'd better go back to work." So I went back to work.

And then it was one of those bad sex times. Lots of talk and not much regularity. Lots of talk like, "Jen, it seems as if I'm just not pleasing you sexually these days."

"Dave, you're just so eager, you just go ahead and do it. I mean, let's be gentle about it."

"Okay, Jen. But I really wish you'd respond more, you know. I mean I'd really like to turn you on."

"Well, it's those soft little touches. They're creepy. I don't know if you want to touch me or if you don't want to touch me. I wish that it would feel like you really felt it and meant it."

"Okay, okay, Jen, I know what you mean, okay.... Well, what happened then?"

"Dave, you're just grabbing me, that's all. I mean, it's me here, not just a body. I'm a person and I want you to respond to me in a personal way."

"But Jen, I really got into it. We like to do that." And finally, "Oh, Jen, can't you just ball! Let's take a shower and ball and have a good time like we used to!"

During this time, I was interested in other women, and every once in a while would have a little thing with somebody. Not often, maybe once or twice a year. It was always a situation where I would just become enthralled and couldn't help myself. I'm not saying that to excuse myself, I'm just stating a fact, that's the way it was. And most of the women I liked to fuck were Jenny's friends. I don't know, Jenny always had wonderful women friends that I always liked and got along with. But you see, the more easily and deeply I fell in love with other women, things at home became more and more tense for me because I was feeling so much guilt. And I couldn't tell her, I couldn't tell her—I didn't tell her.

I finally got involved with somebody bizarre and extraordinary and wonderful and I was really gone. Her name was Charlotte and I met her first with Jenny. I'd heard things about Charlotte, that for a year she has been going out and finding people who are into sadomasochism. Well, one day I was uptown at a gallery with our friend Maria—you remember Maria? We leave the gallery and crossing the street was a gorgeous woman. It's Charlotte. So we all drive downtown together in Maria's car, Charlotte and I are sitting in the back seat and she has some photographs with her and I'm not believing what I am seeing—all these freakish things of people pissing on each other, wax dripping on each other, burning each other's pubic hair. Also some straight bondage fucking, that sort of business. The thing that is interesting about all these things is that Charlotte really went out there and met these people and got involved with them and shot real people who were into that. So I am in the back seat with Charlotte, just feeling the radiance of heat coming off her. And I say, "I'd really like to see you more and fuck you." And she knows that I am in love with her, because I'm just beaming it at her. We have a very deep good-bye kiss in the car and we drop her off and Maria turns to me and says, "You don't miss a trick, do you?"

So I began going over to Charlotte's every day after that and it wasn't just a really good fuck and a nice time. It was crazy! It was fantasy! I had found a female counterpart of myself in terms of fantasy.

But it just got worse, be use I would have a better and better time with Charlotte and a harder and harder time at home. I finally resolved that I was going a little bit out of my mind. All the jobs, Ch rlotte, the school, studio, thinking about art, thinking about how I felt about the art world, thinking about the summer, about land in Maine, worrying about Jenny and wondering where she was all the time, thinking about whether she wanted to fuck or not. Endless! I decided to be through with Charlotte, it's just too unbearable. So one Sunday morning, I got dressed early and went to Charlotte's house. "Look, Charlotte," I said, "we've got to have a different kind of friendship. This can't go on the way we have been going."

And she said, "Okay, okay, but why do you have to be so cool, why do you have to be so cold?"

I said, "I just have to do it like this. I just have to try and cut all of that passion out."

"You don't have to be so unfriendly. You don't have to be so curt. Let's have breakfast."

And I'm thinking, "What are you doing? You're going to have lunch at your mother's in about an hour. You won't be hungry. What are you doing?"

When I saw Jen at my mother's, Jen said, "Where did you go this morning, Dave?"

And I said, "I went over to Charlotte's house."

"Oh, why didn't you tell me?"

"I just don't want to have anything more to do with Charlotte and I sort of needed to do that little chore and not get you involved."

"You could have said something about it."

"I know, I know." And that tension was just singing between us.

Later, on the Staten Island ferry, Jenny said, "This is it. I've had enough. You're just crazy with all that stuff. All the lying and the sneaking around. I just can't take it anymore."

"I know, Jen. Look, I'm not going to do it anymore. I've got to stop."

And I did. I stopped seeing Charlotte. I finished a job in Brooklyn. I started some work in my studio. Things were tense but sort of nice between Jenny and me. I was really working hard at being nice and being good and doing things. I desperately wanted to straighten myself out and I think to me that also meant I would straighten out my relationship with Jenny. But by this time, she had had enough.

You know, after we separated, it struck me that I had heard the phrase "unfaithful" a million times. I've seen films about unfaithful husbands, read books, listened to stories, but I *never* thought of myself as unfaithful. I know I was fucking other women, but I never applied that phrase "adulterer" to myself. I should have, you know. If I had really seen myself in that picture, maybe I would have stopped, but I don't know.

That last summer Jenny went to Maine by herself. I got a letter from her, it was all kind of mixed up: "Dear Dave, I found a beautiful piece of land for us. Did my check arrive? Did Anna call? I miss you and the cat. Love, Jenny." She was gone for weeks and weeks, long after she had said she would be back. I was starved to see her. Then one night, I went with some friends and saw *Scenes from a Marriage*. I came home—Jenny was in the shower. I said, "How are you?"

"Fine." She looks terrific.

"Why don't you come over and give me a kiss?" I stand and watch her shower for a while and then we have a shower together.

"Dave, I can't go on living with you."

"I know, Jenny." Get into bed, kissing, hugging.

"Jenny, I'm really nervous being with you."

"Dave, you're always nervous."

Those first few days I just couldn't grasp the reality of her leaving. Her stuff was here, everything was here. I was just crying all the time. I decided to go up to Vermont for a week and the night I was going to go we got stoned together. All those last conversations were like good-byes. That night

Jenny walked me over to the subway station and we got to the corner of Broadway and Prince and she was going to go over to the grocery to buy cigarettes. And that was the final good-bye, except that was our corner and it will always be our corner, and, of course, we would see each other and we'd be friends.

"I love you, Jen."

"I love you, Dave. But I just can't live with you anymore."

"I know. I know. I haven't made it easy for you."

HOWARD AND FRAN
Chronology

Fall, 1941	**Fran and Howard meet at Temple University.**
Spring, 1942	**They go steady.**
Spring, 1944	**They marry. He lives at Howard University Medical School in Washington and she remains in Philadelphia.**
1947	**Sara is born.**
1949	**Lena is born.**
1954	**They move to St. Louis. Howard becomes assistant professor of psychiatry at George Washington University.**
1957	**They buy their house.**
1963	**Fran goes back to school for a master's in psychology.**
1973	**Fran and Howie separate.**

4
The Worshiper
and the Worshipee

The Worshiper-Worshipee marriage myth is the most enduring of them all. It promises to provide the ideal balance between a man and a woman. In this marriage, the husband provides his wife with the security that all her needs will be taken care of and that he will share his personal success with her. And the wife provides her husband with the comforts of a warm and efficiently run home, well-brought-up children, and emotional support. It really appears to be the perfect arrangement for mutual fulfillment.

When Howard and Fran Rawlins met over thirty years ago, they saw they could give each other the love and security that makes for a complete and enduring marriage.

A black man of West Indian heritage, Howard Rawlins grew up as the only child of a middle-class family in Philadelphia. Now, at fifty-three, he is a prominent psychiatrist and university professor living alone in a St. Louis suburb. He is fairly short and well-built, with a light complexion and receding brown hair. Dr. Rawlins is an entertaining talker, mixing West Indian metaphors with the jargon of his profession and the Yiddish of his childhood neighborhood.

HOWIE:

I remember when I was an early teenager, my father used to say, "Son, passion is wonderful. Good sense is another thing. And in most instances in life they are inimical to each other. One is indeed fortunate if one has both passion and tenderness in the love object, but don't you ever let your dick lead you into a life situation that's impossible."

I had my first sexual experience at about fifteen and I never gave a serious thought to marriage. But I think that I really first fell in love with Frances. It was the first time I had encountered the combination of lust and tenderness in a woman, and it was new to me.

I met Fran in an anthropology classroom at Temple University in the fall of, I believe, 1941. She was sitting a row in front of me. I was attracted to her because she seemed somewhat of an exotic Sicilian or Spanish beauty. As a matter of fact, I didn't even know that she was colored at the time. In my family it was understood that you didn't get involved with any woman on a marital level unless your children could be both bright and attractive—and in those days part of being attractive was being light.

My mother and father got along with Fran instantly. She immediately started calling my mother "Mama," about which I had certain mixed feelings *(laughs)*. I was an only child and it was almost as if I had gone out in the world and dredged up the daughter that my mother always wished she'd had. I had a dog at the time named Spike and a cat named Guzzy, and the dog and the cat took to her too! *(laughs)*.

Gradually, Fran and I became very close. Young, green, dumb as I was, I wasn't so crazy. I always had sense for, you know, substantial women. Women whose character was decent. I could never marry a woman for pussy. The idea of that is anathema to me. Fucking 'em is one thing. Marrying them is another. I think the kind of women you go out with is a reflection of what you think of yourself. I was always proud of Fran. She had taste and a sense of social awareness. I didn't worry that she'd do something off the wall. So all things considered, I considered myself very lucky. I also considered *her* very lucky.

I wanted to be a doctor from the time I can recall. To me it was just a matter of an arrow leaving a bow and going on target. I knew just what my life was going to be and I was pursuing it. I was going to Washington, D.C., to Howard University Medical School.

Medical school turned out to be a really fortuitous turning point in my life because I realized for the first time that I had the unconscious notion that only white men had brains and were competent—except for my father and our doctor. At Howard for the first time in my life I met a large number of extremely competent, extremely bright black men and my eyes opened to the trick bag that this goddamn racist society had put on me. I was very impressed by another phenomenon at the time: Generally speaking, the faculty of the medical school were all rather handsome, very bright, fair-complected Negro men who had what they used to call "good hair"—that is to say, wavy, nonkinky hair. They were married in most cases to good-looking women who were indistinguishable from white and who had gone to various posh schools, Holyoke, Smith, places like that. And looking at my own self it seemed as though I was just fitting into the same pattern. Fran was a very pretty, bright, nice-looking woman. Everybody thought that we were well suited to each other in every possible way. We were like, you know, a golden couple.

I have one memory of our wedding night and it's a miracle I've not become a leader of the Symbionese Liberation Army because of it. I had made reservations for us to spend our wedding night at the Roosevelt Hotel in New York. I should add that I had been taken into the Army

Specialized Training Program in September of my fresh-
man year in med school. When we got to the hotel, the desk
clerk said—and I was wearing my uniform of the United
States Army—that they didn't take Negroes in the hotel.
The first night with my wife! I really never wanted to commit murder like I did that night. We left there and went to
Harlem, the Theresa was filled, so we went around the
corner to another hotel. The next morning we drove up to
Nyack, New York, and for the first time in my life I was
impotent. The whole honeymoon was a disaster.

Fran got a job in the VA in Philadelphia. She stayed
there so I could dedicate myself to my studies. I'd go home
from school on the weekends and she would occasionally
come down to dances. My parents moved in with Fran and
they got along like three peas in a pod. When I came home,
there'd be a great deal of affection. Fran used to sit in my
lap in the rocker and we used to talk baby talk to each other.
I was really quite happy with her. It was that normal insanity called love which fortunately we all recover from.

Somehow I always felt that it was ridiculous to believe
that when you got married, you'd be blind to somebody
else. You can love your wife and screw somebody else and it
doesn't mean that you don't love you wife. That's life.
When I was in college and studying a great deal, I really
wasn't looking around. But after getting married and re-
turning to medical school, I decided to experiment sexually.
I met a girl who was about eighteen or nineteen and she was
a real knockout: one of these kind of reddish, yam-colored
black women with wavy auburn hair. I made it very clear to
her that I was married and wasn't interested in anything
serious, which I wasn't. When Fran found out, she was, of
course, extremely upset and I was upset myself.

But women center much more on their sex lives than I
do. To me, the most important thing in the world was
hacking it professionally and nothing would stand in the
way of that. My reputation as being a very competent,

extremely capable physician always came first and then came wife, family, and so forth. There was no question that I was a source of pride for Fran in that regard.

When Fran announced she was pregnant, it upset the bejesus out of me. I suddenly felt like my freedom had been foreclosed. But I was astonished when I found myself eagerly looking forward to putting my ear to her belly to listen to the movements of Sara. Occasionally her foot or her arm or something would punch me on the cheek, and I would have conversations with Sara while she was in utero. I had not made a really mature visceral connection between the idea of sex and having kids, and it was fascinating. Now I looked forward to it.

Sara became the apple of my eye and still is to this day. I really was wonderfully attached to her from the start but I was in for another blow. When I brought Fran and Sara home it seemed as though they had formed a unit unto themselves and all I was important for was to provide them with food and shelter and whatever money was necessary. I felt very excluded. I can remember really getting very angry at the sight of Fran nursing Sara, the two of them so happy together while I was left out. Meanwhile I had met a nurse at the hospital where I had just started my residency. Looking back now, I think my behavior really was saying, "Well, Fran, if you're going to leave me for this baby slurping up all of this milk, I'm going to find me somebody to give me some attention." The nurse was the greatest sexual partner I've ever had in my life—I really achieved genital maturity with her—but I never would have abandoned my wife and kid for anybody or anything. As a matter of fact, I'd do much more for somebody who I loved affectionately than for somebody who I loved erotically.

Nine months after Sara was born, Fran announced that she was pregnant with Lenie. I was really angry with myself again. I said to myself that a man's dick sure can get him in a lot of goddamned trouble; it can simultaneously be the source of the greatest satisfaction and the greatest *tsuris*.

Fran went to her mother's in California to hatch Lenie and it was like water falling off a duck's back. I have the happiest memories of Fran and me bathing Lenie and Sara and taking pictures of them in the tub. I'd kiss them on their butts and put Johnson's baby powder on them and they were warm and cuddly and responsive. They were beautiful kids and I was very pleased and proud of them.

When we first came to St. Louis it was really like a new beginning. I can honestly say this was the golden age of our marriage. For the first time we were free of family, just us and the kids living alone. It really was a new beginning. Both of us felt a certain optimism. I was very pleased with the direction of my life, and I was getting someplace. You know, I was a first-generation American and the first year in practice I made $13,000 and the second I made like $35,000. We started saving money toward buying a house. We practically had to fight the goddamn war all over again to get the goddamned house. One of my psychiatrist colleagues wouldn't let us buy his; he said to me: "Oh, we signed a nonaggression pact with our neighbors that no undesirables would live in the neighborhood." So we got this Jewish lawyer to buy an acre of land for us as a strawman and we built a gorgeous $60,000 house on a very fancy street. The kids could walk to the public school around the corner.

Oh, Fran and I had a lot of fun together in those days. I remember I bought her her first car and she was scared to death to learn to drive. And my mother used to come and visit and we loved to have her. I used to like to play with the kids and take them for rides on Sunday. We'd have a great time. The girls and I would go and get Fran birthday presents and anniversary presents and Christmas presents and Easter presents. We'd go and get her flowers, which I did all through our marriage.

During that golden period I can remember looking forward to going home. One of the great joys was being met at the door by the dog and the girls all jumping up to be kissed and hugged one at a time. Fran would always have the kids wait for me because she knew that was the way I was brought up; that was the way it was supposed to be. The family waited on the father to come home and we'd all sit down at the table together, just shy of setting a place for the dog. I used to tell Fran, "In this household, I am the Sun and you and the children and the dog my moons, my Saturns, my satellites. I am the center of this house. This family falls apart without me." My father said the man is supposed to be the head of the household to the extent that he can and I was always very glad that I could. And Fran was truly a superwife—a tremendous housekeeper, a tremendous cook, a tremendously good mother. I would never dream of anything else. That's the way it was with my father and mother.

The golden age came to an end with the advent of the children's puberty. I'm sure what was going on was stirring Fran and me up and bringing up our own adolescence, and gradually I noticed that I was beginning to develop a feeling to Fran more like she was a sister than a lover—the lust wasn't there. We were getting to be more and more like Hansel and Gretel, just moving imperceptibly in that direction, and I knew fucking well that there was nothing so odd about me. It's not some unique thing. I think this happens in every marriage, but it is amazing to me that I have never seen a paper on this phenomenon by a psychiatrist. I suspect the sons of bitches unconsciously avoid this crucial human problem.

Why is it that when people are tremendously drawn to each other and have the best of both worlds—lust and affection—gradually, if they are lucky, only affection remains? We *were* affectionate, we'd hug and kiss each other; I just didn't feel any lust for her. That's really the reason why we were divorced. I refuse to go to bed with woman "A" and have fantasies of woman "X" in order to function with woman "A." I told Fran, "Look, I don't know what the hell is going on. I care for you very, very much. There's nothing I wouldn't do for you, but I can't make believe. . . ." And she said, "Listen, this goddamn brother-and-sister relationship we have is for the birds. You're impotent with me." I said, "What is a man, a fucking machine?"

Well, about a year and half before we separated, Fran told me that it was too frustrating to share a bed with me anymore and she announced she was going to move into one of the other bedrooms. I mean, I used to cuddle with her and all that—Fran is a very cuddlesome, warm, soft woman—but she said it is too frustrating. I said, "What do you want to do that for? Why are you cutting off your nose to spite your face?" That really upset me because I knew that was the beginning of the end.

We weren't really fighting. It was a kind of sadness. And I do think that the girls reaching puberty had something to do with it. Sara and Lenie both grew into very pretty young women and one of Fran's greatest delights was when they started to date; she would be dressing them, checking their lipstick and eye shadow, and then she'd wait up for them until they came back from a dance or a party and they'd all stay up and talk. It was as if Fran was sort of living out her own dating. I didn't really want to sit up and talk to them about what they did but at the same time it sort of pissed me off that she had some sort of special thing with them. She always referred to them as "my girls." And occasionally I'd scream, "I suppose you had these kids by parthenogenesis while I'm breaking my ass to supply them with everything."

Fran was always dependent, and you know, that is a two-edged sword. I can distinctly remember getting up on cold winter mornings when she'd be still sacked out and the dog would jump in the bed as I got out of it. I'd be getting dressed to go to work and I'd say, "Look at her and the mutt." Oh sure, I used to bitch and moan and groan, "Well, the least you can do is get up and get my breakfast," and she'd say, "But you don't eat breakfast." Outside of orange juice and a cup of coffee I didn't eat breakfast and I suppose my bitching was really to get her ass out of the bed so I wouldn't be walking around in the cold all alone.

When Fran started to get her master's degree, that really turned the equilibrium of the marriage upside down. She was busy studying and running the house too and I had to do a lot more things than previously. As she went to work she started to get more and more independent, and frankly, one of the things that was gradually pissing me off through the years was that not only was I supporting the whole household, lock, stock, and barrel, but shit, I started coming home and I'd be cooking dinner too. I began to say to myself, "Turkey! What is this, clown? Here you are taking care of the whole shebang—you buy all the food, you pay all the goddamn utilities, the mortgage, and you've got a wife who spends money like it's going out of style—and here you are cooking your own dinner!" I said to Fran several times, "What's with you? You've got the original husband. What is this shit?"

I think I had some premonitions that when the kids left we might go apart; they had a binding effect and when they disappeared there wasn't enough there to hold us together. It was agonizing to think about giving up the house because it was so full of memories. I never envisaged really breaking with Fran. My mother had made it very clear to me that no one in our family had ever gotten divorced and people who did lacked character, were low-lifes. I told Fran, "Listen, I don't need some goddamned divorce. I don't want to marry somebody else." And she said, "Look, why protract this brother-and-sister thing—this asexuality?" So we had what amounted to a very civilized divorce.

I have no regrets. Not one. You know that old girlfriend I mentioned, the nurse? She married some old boyfriend and it's like my father used to tell me as a very young man—that I should look at a woman to see if I could predict what she'd look like in fifteen years. Sure enough, I saw this woman recently and said to myself, "Oh, boy, you were right, guy." She had grown from a sexy thing to a roll of fat. I wouldn't hit a dog in the ass with her now. Young and dumb as I was, I had wonderful judgment in picking Frances as a mate. At fifty-one she's a much better-appearing person and there's just more depth to her.

Yes, Frances is a warm woman and a good person and I liked my relationship with her. But that doesn't mean I'm going to get remarried and you'd better believe that I'd shack up with somebody for a period of time before I made that decision again. What happens in bed is one thing and what happens out of bed is where we spend most of our time and is much more important in life.

It's funny, since I've been single I've met a couple of young women, widows and divorceés who have little children, and these women exercise a fantastic appeal to me. I don't mean the woman per se, it's the child, the dog, the woman, and the house. It's a gestalt and I'm sure it has something to do with wanting to relive that golden age of Frances and me and our kids and the dog. It has a sentimental, schmaltzy appeal, but I know that the fantasy would come apart like peanut brittle hit with a hammer if it was every day, "Daddy, I wanna drink of water," and "What about the baby-sitter?" and again with the department store bills and the college tuition.

You know, I think that if Fran and I were poorer, we'd probably still be together, living a sort of quiet but very affectionate desperation. It's twenty-nine, just short of thirty years since we married. Right up to our *senium*. That's a long time.

At fifty-one, Frances Rawlins is an unusually sexy-looking woman. She is slim, with a youthful face and full, black hair. Mrs. Rawlins grew up in Philadelphia in a lower-mid-

dle-class black American family and completed her educa-
tion with a master's degree in psychology at George
Washington University in St. Louis, where she now lives.
She is a warm person and an animated talker with a
frequent, luxuriant laugh.

FRAN:

I had boyfriends since I was eleven years old. My mother used to say, "I hope Fran gets married early." I played spin the bottle and post office, and then as I got a little older I was always in the hallways of the apartment building. Someone always would tell my mother that Fran was necking in the hallway. But that's all it was. I was just a flirt until I went to college, and that's when Howie grabbed hold of me fast.

I remember the first time I saw him, I said to myself, "Boy, what an aggressive guy!" He sat next to me in anthropology class and said, "Do you have the text?" I said, "Not here," so he said he'd come home with me to borrow it. That's Howie. I sort of said, "Wow!"

We went home together and he met my mother and sister and amused them. He's so charming and funny, but my first reaction was, "It's too much." Anyway, there was somebody else in my life, Johnny, who was a real nut and very handsome. Nothing but trouble, but I was very taken with him.

Howie pursued me anyway, really sort of overwhelming in his pursuit. He went home with me every day. And I had never met anyone quite as brilliant as he was. I admired his stability in school because I was a very erratic student. I had no goals, but he always knew what he wanted to do: to be a doctor. He was on top of his life and that was so appealing, especially compared to Johnny. There was no future there. Howie's occupation in the lunchroom was to tease me about Johnny—"The Truck Driver," he called him—and that is what Johnny became after they threw him out of the third college.

I wasn't initially attracted to Howie, not even physically. Johnny was six-foot-one and he was only five-foot-seven. I loved Howie for different things. I admired him. The relationship with Johnny just petered out—and there was Howie. I really grew to like him. He was demonstrative and sentimental.

But I have to be perfectly honest and say that it wasn't until after Howie and I had sex that I fell in love with him. It was such a gratifying sexual experience. I was scared to death—I was eighteen and a half—but he was affectionate and tender. He was very good and I discovered that I was very sexy. It was amazing the way it happened. He didn't have to talk me into it at all. Just one day—I knew it. And he knew it. Nothing was said. He picked me up and took me to one of those little hotels downtown and that was it. I loved it. I had been asked by other guys and it had always been "No," but Howie never asked. He was very dominating and I was attracted to that. I needed it, I guess. So we began having sexual experiences and I was falling madly in love with him. It was so gratifying to at last have a genital sexual relationship because I had done a heck of a lot of masturbation, in latency even. This was the first time I had a totally satisfying thing.

I really went into Howie's world. I found myself with Howie's friends; they were much more intellectual than mine. The few people I maintained my own friendships with were people he would tolerate. We loved jazz, used to dance a lot and go to parties a lot. I was very warm and very giving and I admired him. The most obvious thing about our relationship was that we meshed well: He seemed to adore me and I was crazy about him. It reached the point where people used to laugh at us—the lovers, inseparable and stuff.

By this time he was in medical school. I was so impressed with him. I was in awe, in a way. Boy—here he is, he gets out of high school in three and a half years, he gets out of college, he gets accepted to medical school! It was difficult to get accepted by a medical school if you're black. He went off to Washington while I stayed in Philadelphia and finished college. I remember during the end of that year my aunt invited me to spend the summer in California. That was sort of exciting and I wrote him that I had mixed feelings about going. He wrote me back, how could I think about going away? It was very poignant and very open in his feelings toward me. Isn't that funny? I saved that letter for years. But I tore up all those old things before the divorce.

I became so dependent on him—for sleeping together, for my friends, for some stability in my life. I didn't bring up marriage first, he did. He said, "Should we wait until I get out of school?" And I said, "Why? That's four more years." He was scared, but he married me because he loved me and he didn't want to lose me. I wanted to get married because I just wanted to legitimize our sex. He made me feel so secure and safe, I knew our marriage was going to be fine. It was going to be like the fairy stories. He would take care of everything and I would take care of his emotional needs; I'm a very supportive-type person, I'm patient. I could sit down and listen to him if anything went wrong; he could ventilate these things. Howie has always been a worrier and I'd calm him down, pet him and so forth. Like he was afraid if he got married, his career was going out the window. Medical students didn't get married in those days. He was worried about the responsibility. "What do you mean?" I'd say. "I'm going to work." I understood where he was at and I told him that it would be all right. And that was the way I was almost all throughout the marriage. "This will pass, it'll be all right, don't worry, Howie." I'd have to calm him down and get him past the crisis.

So we went ahead. I had no feelings about being a married lady, just that now we could be together openly. Well, the shit hit the fan right away. We had registered at a hotel in New York and this hotel did not honor our reservations because we were black. I felt so sorry for Howie. What a put-down for him. We slept together, but it wasn't like it was. I could understand it, of course. He was angry, he was furious, and he was hurt.

Howie set it up after we were married that he would be in Washington and I would stay in Philadelphia with his parents. That's another thing, Howie's mother. When I met that lady, I fell in love with her. She was from the West Indies and had a very cultured accent. A tall, very elegant-looking lady with a wonderful sense of humor. She was crazy about me and I was crazy about her. It was just one of those things. There was nothing she wouldn't do for me. And Howie was jealous. When we moved to St. Louis and the dean of psychiatry came over, Howie introduced Mama and said, "This is why Fran married me" (laughs).

Then I discovered that Howie had an affair. A girl friend of mine told me. I was so hurt, I just couldn't believe it. I thought we were so close. I confronted him and at first he denied it, but then he told me. His ego is such that when he wants something, that's it. But he loved me always, even when he was having an affair. I met this girl and she said that he spent most of the time talking about me and how great I am! Talk about chutzpah! Howie had it. We talked about this affair. I was upset, but I wanted to stay married. Howie was my life.

Then the desire to have children became overwhelming. He's still in medical school and I'm suffering over this affair. All of a sudden I started saying to myself, "How do I know I can have kids?" An obsession. But I never tricked Howie in terms of saying, "I'm safe," when I wasn't. He knew I didn't have a diaphragm on once and he wanted the kid. But once I was pregnant, he started having an affair with a nurse. But then I had Sara and I was thrilled. Howie was thrilled too. She was a beautiful baby, healthy-looking, robust, bright, and laughed a lot. And my feeling about

Howie was, "Howie will grow up when he realizes that nothing will interfere with his getting what he wants." He was the most steadfast person when it came to his profession, but in his emotional life he was a baby. He was always anxious. but I still loved him and needed him. We were happy.

Then I got pregnant with Lenie and he became a monster. I knew he was going to be upset—but I was doing my own thing by this time and I wasn't paying any attention to him. I realized that the family is going to be me and my kids and he's going to be apart from it. And I would have to work around him instead of this sort of mutual relationship we'd had earlier. Things were pretty bad for a while there. I even had a little affair and told Howie about it. I said to myself that I was being honest, but I really wanted to hurt him.

And then we finally got a break. Howie decided to move to St. Louis and I decided on my own to give it a good try. You know, we really never had a chance, we really never led a real life in terms of living together—either he was in medical school and I was up in Philadelphia or he was in residency and never home. He started his psychiatric training again in St. Louis and those were the best years we ever had. First of all, I felt the support of his therapist, who happened to be a female, a Viennese woman. So Howie had another female he was seeing three days a week, but it wasn't an affair! (laughs).

In those years, I felt so good about the marriage. I loved him, of course, and he loved me. Even through those affairs he had, he never stopped loving me. We'd go on vacations, we'd have fun, we'd laugh a lot, we'd talk a lot. I used to read all his books and we would talk about his work a lot. The sex would be good. We were both cuddlers. At night, if I was angry with him I would not go to bed because Howie was very soft and if I got close to him, I'd find myself cuddling (laughs). And then that would lead to something else and I'd say, "Goddamn it!" I'm a very sensuous person and that would be my downfall (laughs).

We decided that we were going to build a house, and that took a long time and a lot of energy. That house was expensive, thousands of dollars, and Howie paid everything. He used to call himself a workhorse 'cause he had to pay for everything. But he's still a workhorse and he doesn't have to support anybody. Now he says he has to work hard to pay me my $350 alimony (*laughs*).

We were a charming couple then. We both made a lot of friends. People liked us and they loved to come to our home. There was good food, good conversation, a lot of fun. Howie was very proud of the way I entertained. I would cook and he would serve drinks. I think our friends knew how difficult he was, but they probably felt I handled him well. There would be times when Howie would be impossible, but my timing was always such that I knew when and how to deal with it. I was not passive in my relationship to him, but on the other hand Howie would be the one to handle things. He just did things and he wouldn't even talk to me about them. Autombiles? He bought automobiles, period. Did I want blue maybe? Nothing. I used to be embarrassed Christmastime when people would come to the house and see all the presents under the tree. It looked like a department store window.

Howie was a responsible husband and father. He earned a living and he did care for us. And how he loved Sara! To the exclusion of Lenie. Lenie was a delightful little girl, but from the beginning he said, "She isn't going to amount to anything." All he would see was that Sara was a princess and Lenie was a fuck-up. Sara says that she is the favorite because it was a narcissistic choice of Howie's. She was the student like Howie. I don't think he was a good father. He put in time and money. but he didn't give of himself. He lectured. He never talked. He knew I raised the girls. On the emotional level of the marriage, I kept things calm; that was me—stabilizing the emotional climate in the house. But he didn't think those things were as important as what he did—earning money and working.

Howie was a very complex person, like Dr. Jekyll and Mr. Hyde. He has such energy and when he would get angry, you could feel this energy get out. He never hit anybody, but the things he would say. Put-downs. Loud bellows. His work was totally different. He worked hard and he was always on top of that, but when he'd walk home he'd leave all that knowledge and patience in the office and I'd say, "Here comes Howie, the truck driver."

Sure, he was very sentimental, but it was a substitute for deeper feelings. He never cried in front of me, and when I needed his support, forget it. For example, he couldn't tolerate my being sick. When he was sick, of course, he liked to be catered to. But I had surgery twice and I remember my surgeon saying after each operation, "You gotta be strong for Howie." I thought a man who was stable in his work and could support you was a man of strong character. But that isn't necessarily true. It wasn't true of Howie.

Finally, I decided that I wanted to be my own person. The girls were getting older. I wanted to do something else so I applied to school to get a master's in psychology. Howie always said that it was as important for girls to be well educated as men, so when I told him, he said, "Fine!" But he didn't like it. It was a change in the routine at home and the house wasn't run the way it used to be. The girls were great. They said I should have gone back to school years ago. But Howie never asked to look at a paper of mine or anything. I knew he had mixed feelings about it. I think I always made sacrifices for my marriage, to keep it going. But I'm not aware of any compromises that Howie was really willing to make. Maybe he did, but I'm not aware of them.

And yet he was always proud of me and my interests. He would tease me, but he was proud that I did so well at school. He taught a course in the Psychology Department while I was there. He's a great teacher, of course. He used to call on all of my friends, but he knew he better not call on me (*laughs*), He got angry that I got an A in his course and I didn't study for the exam (*laughs*). It was an objective test, by the way.

And then our sex life gradually got to be horrible. He began not to be interested in sex at all. We'd talk about it and he said he was beginning to feel like I'm a sister. This all coincided with my doing more of my own thing, feeling great about myself and going back to school. I think I was starting to intimidate him. And he picked that area—he knows I'm a passionate person—to deprive me. I don't know if it was conscious or unconscious. Who cares? I was not going to live that way. It was so clearly his anger. But all his knowledge went out the window. Bad sex is a symptom, Howie of all people should have known that. I started thinking about having an affair. Constantly. Fantasying. But you know, I have teenage kids, I have a position in the community. Who was I going to have an affair with? And Howie was so protective of me that anyone who knew him would never approach me. So I just went back to my masturbation.

Howie always loved women, though. There was nothing he liked better than to be surrounded by them. There were times when we lived in the house and Howie was at the head of the table and I'd be at the other end and there would be all women in between us, my girls, friends—he loved it! And we'd all laugh at him and argue with him, they'd tell him how impossible he is, but he was there—he was the center! He still has a charm about him. He really does. When you don't have to live with him and go through the pain of his narcissism and insensitivity, when you know him on this kind of level and not the most intimate level, he's fine. His charming personality—that aggression, that domination —there is nothing charming about it if you live with it. Maybe I loved that once, but I guess it's like they say in the trade—I decathected. That appeal died.

I was scared, but one day I sat myself down and said, "Come on, Fran, you're a big girl. You know you've got a lot of strength, you can do it." And I told Howie that we've got to separate. And he agreed, but he didn't do anything. By this time, I was sleeping in the guest room, I was taking vacations by myself and having affairs. It was just procrastination. Then I went to Puerto Rico and he wrote to me and said he didn't want a divorce. I wrote back, "But this is where we are. There's nothing left." And he said—get the logic of this—that I must care for him because he couldn't care for me unless he knew I cared for him. He is such an egomaniac and I was hating it by this time. On the other hand, if Howie hadn't had such an ego and drive to succeed, I—well—I wouldn't have been married to him. I told you what I had been attracted to—his success, his stability. That's why I'm not angry at Howie, I just don't want to see him much.

I've grown a lot since the divorce. I've certainly grown sexually. I have good sexual partners now. I remember I met this guy in Puerto Rico who used to live in St. Louis and now lives in New York. I used to fly to New York to visit him. And it was the first time a guy fixed meals for me. I said, "Wow! Isn't this great!" It was so intimate. You know, you can assure continuity in marriage but you can never assure the continuity of intimacy.

I have no regrets. Not once have I been sorry that I terminated the relationship with Howie. It's like that Martin Luther King thing. Free at last! Free at last! Why did I wait so long?

CESAR AND AMY
Chronology

1967	Cesar and Amy meet in Miami, Florida. Within three months, they marry.
1967–68	They live in the East Village, New York City.
1968–69	They live in Florida.
1969	They are busted in a drug raid.
1970	Sasha is born.
1971	They move to Brooklyn, New York.
1972	Sasha becomes seriously ill.
1972	They move to New Hope, Pennsylvania.
1972	Krishna is born.
1974	They separate.

5

The Spiritual Marriage

One of the most popular myths of recent years is that of the Spiritual Marriage. United by a shared spiritual awareness, this couple seeks a pure life liberated from the egotism of the materialist world. They are always searching for new levels of transcendence and new ways to grow. Together, they exude a oneness-with-life that intoxicates everyone around them. They are attached to nothing in the world, except each other.

Cesar Cortazar and Amy Phillips met each other in the early stages of their quest for a purer life and were drawn to each other's spirituality.

Cesar Cortazar is an unusually handsome and mystical-looking young man. His silky black hair hangs to his shoulders and his dark, heavy-lidded eyes verge on the hypnotic. Yet for all his intensity, this twenty-five-year-old Cuban-born American is an easy, humorous talker who recreates scenes complete with caricatured accents. At present, Cesar is unemployed and lives with a group of friends in New Hope, Pennsylvania, less than one mile from his former wife and their children.

CESAR:

I came into Miami to try to get some money from the Veterans Adminstration for this Summerhill school I was going to set up in central Florida. I had taken my six-line hookah and my oso smoke with me to turn people on that I was meeting during the day. I went with my friend Omar to an apartment in Miami Beach where his girl had been staying, and he introduced me to her friend, Amy. Amy and I made a solid connection immediately. She seemed refreshing and healthy and light and just felt good.

We had dinner and I think we made love and after I left that evening I wanted to get in touch with her again. I called but she wasn't there. It seemed she had been taken away by the local sheriff for not paying the bill at some motel someplace. I wanted to call her because I wanted to ask her to marry me (*laughs*). I was very romantically inclined and marriage always seemed very important to me. I fell in love easily with many people—I still do, but now I don't ask them to marry me (*laughs*). With Amy it was different. You see, Amy had just been into a heavy drug scene with cocaine and speed and she'd kind of taken off to recuperate and gotten into a new spiritual group. She had found Meher Baba. So, like, her whole personality was lightening up because of this spiritual quest, and I liked that lightness.

The next morning I was trying to get money together to spring Amy, but by the time I got there she was out already. Somewhere along the line I asked her to marry me and she thought I was crazy. I said, "You don't have to make up your mind right away. Just think about it." She did and we just hung out together.

One of the greatest things bringing us together at that time was Meher Baba. I'd touched on Baba while I was at the Cayce Center, and when I first saw how much Amy admired him, it was making me jealous. I used to get rid of his pictures and didn't want to read any of his books. But then I did and some of them were intensely light, if the paradox makes sense to you. Intensely light.

We went to the Grove one evening and some male energy tried to pull Amy away, but she decided she wanted to stick with me. That made me feel good and sometime that evening we decided that maybe it would be a good union.

We were married in a county courthouse. Just simple. There was enough celebration between the two of us that it just didn't matter. And our plans were left in the hands of Providence. We had taken on a spiritual quest to be blown, like dust, wherever we might land. We felt that as long as we had each other, we were basically all right. There was just this whole hope that was flowing through us, you see. As long as we kept this flow going, we were always happy, always protected. We decided that we would try to take control of nothing and work toward liberating ourselves of what is called false ego.

So we went up to New York and stopped along the way to visit Amy's mother. She had known I was Cuban, but when she saw me with my hair halfway down my back and almost charred black from the Florida sun, she turned from white to transparent (*laughs*). So we continued on our "Journey to the East," and ended up on the Lower East Side of Manhattan (*laughs*). That was around *Sergeant Pepper* time. A lot of magic. Magic people. Drugs were free if you were into the right connections with people, the right vibrations. It was a veritable Mecca. You'd walk in past the first landing of this eight-flight walk-up and you'd get stoned just from the vapors in the hallway. We were shooting up Methedrine and acid, but we felt that there was a purpose in it. Somehow we weren't having all the fun trips that everybody else was having, because we kept very light air. While we were wired out on speed we were always rapping to people about Baba and it kind of quieted everybody down. We opened up our home all the time to people to get themselves cooled out. And we would make them feel better. I guess Amy and I projected something like Krishnarada. We were like this couple who were the male and female counterparts of universal energy, working toward something good that people liked.

There was a day on which we observed silence in honor of Baba and that evening we took a walk into Tompkins Square Park. This girl started to talk to us and we wouldn't talk back. She thought we were such sweet mute children. She wanted to take us home with her. She said, "What are you kids doing here late at night in Tompkins Square Park? I'll take you someplace where it's safe." Those were the kinds of experiences we were having in the city.

But the more we got into drugs, the heavier it got and the harder to cope with the external as well as the internal. You know, speed is a very strong physical condition. We were starting to go crazy—we were getting reconditioned to a very negative kind of energy. Our body, our vehicle, was unable to cope. Amy was beginning to imagine people tapping her on the shoulder and voices going past and I saw we were going to get really jammed there, and we had to get out of this environment. Amy didn't want to leave, so I had to fabricate a whole paranoid situation that there were people who were after us and we had to get out of town or they'd get us. Evil spirits. I didn't have the energy to reason with her—it was for her own good. So we got it together and made it down to Florida.

From the point where we start doing speed, our innocence starts to disappear and I become much more oppressive. I feel a kind of pressure down inside—I feel her clinging. Not giving me space to be myself. Cutting me down when I don't wish to be pursued. It always happens at the moment when she is feeling insecure about something and she is thinking, "I'm going to test him. I'm going to see how much he loves me." And so it's, "Cesar, will you do the dishes? If you loved me, you'd do the dishes."

"Oh, but I'm really tired, and really, my head's not into it."

"If you really loved me, you'd do the dishes."

"I do love you."

"Then why won't you do the dishes?" She gets hysterical and we have a fight. I don't want to listen to her and I don't want to get to the part where we'll be at each other's throats. But the Baba helped to resolve our problems.

You see, this kind of pettiness is a typical position on the path of spiritual development and we did not want to succumb to worldly drunkenness. The Baba showed us we could get beyond this.

I was working at a head shop on Biscayne Boulevard in Miami. I had the leather concession. At the time we were between places and we had some friends who played in a rock band who said, "Why don't you come and stay with us while you are looking for a place to stay?" So we did.

The place was really nutty, all kinds of things going on. Like in the kitchen there was a shooting gallery, mad sex in the bedrooms, all kinds of crazy traffic running in and out, and music all hours of the night. There were all these heads in funny places. And Amy and I gave this sensation of intoxication to people. We had the kind of love that in the midst of confusion comes shining through with selflessness and understanding. There was an aura we gave off, a joy and a communion, not just between the two of us, but with everything around us. Some people wished to try to idolize us and make us into saints, so, like, we were always trying to tell people that turn to us, "Hey, man, it's not just us, it's you, it's the same thing. Don't make us out to be more than we really are because we are only extensions of yourself." You see, if you allow people to keep focusing themselves on you, it starts to become a drain on you. That's why you use Baba as a universal focal point. One week most of the boys in the rock band went off to the Baba Center in Myrtle Beach because of us.

So the boys were gone and one day this girl we thought was a groupie came along and she wanted to score some smoke. We weren't into that much at the time, but I had some things I had to deliver around town, some sandals and a harness for an armadillo, so I said if she'd take us around town, maybe one place or another she could get an ounce of something.

We went to this one place and I was fitting the armadillo for a harness there when she scored. Then this girl said, "I've got to go outside and call up my mother," something about keeping the car out too long. Ten minutes later there's this knocking at the door and she says it's her. Amy and I open the door and three armed men come bashing through with guns with great big barrels. A bust! The armadillo ran under the bed, he was scared by the vibrations. We were handcuffed and sat on the bed and they asked us all sorts of questions. There wasn't much to find, just a couple of pounds.

While two of the policemen are rummaging around the house, one comes to our attaché valise and starts to open it up, but before he does he says, "What's in there?" And I said, "My Baba literature." We carried it with us everywhere, like Jehovah's Witnesses. And this guy says, "What's a Baba?" To which the hipper detective said, "Oh, you can leave that stuff alone." And they never did look in that case. Automatically, Baba meant something to him and he just trusted whatever was in there. Through all this, Amy and I didn't even care. It was an inconvenience, but we were trying to see what Baba was trying to tell us through this. That was our concern.

We were booked and that night we managed to get on the six o'clock news—they really played us up as part of a major narcotics ring (laughs). Anyway, that evening someone rattles my cage and says, "Okay, somebody sprung you." The syndicate? (laughs). No, my mother. My first thought wasn't just to get out, it was to get under the mattress and grab all the chocolate bars and cookies I'd been given for rolling cigarettes for the guys and redistribute them to the other people who needed them.

So Amy and I were out on probation, working in a head shop—my probation officer didn't find that objectionable (*laughs*)—keeping our noses clean, smoking good dope, making love, being happy. I taught Amy the embellishments of cookery: That was a turn-on for her. And then Amy had Sasha—it always seemed a pretty name for a boy and I figured in years to come, as he grows fine and sexy, it will be a boon to him. For a while there, we kept pretty much to ourselves, stuffing our faces and watching TV together.

But you know, Amy and I always had a few skirmishes. And one of the focal points, I remember, is Amy didn't like the idea of me having any kind of interest, mental, physical, or spiritual, in another woman. The question would always come up, "Do you find her prettier than me? Do you like her better than me? Would you rather be with her?" You know, those loaded questions. They put you on the spot. Her questions are If and And and Or kind of questions, ultimate black-and-white kinds of questions—"If you like her, you can't like me." It was like a demand and it turned me off. And I just couldn't, in my deepest sensibilities, do that to myself—just start making myself feel turned off to everyone. It became very unhealthy. Because I was being told not to, I wanted to do more. So finally I said to myself, "This is ridiculous—slinking around, making sure that she's not looking, being paranoid all the time. I'll just be blatant about it and show her, 'This is the way I am. You don't like it? Well, take a walk, man, because I can't live like that.' "

But she's got this nagging quality about her. She picks something up. she won't let it go. She follows me around; she won't let me alone, and I say, "Please, give me some space. Let me get my head together. I can't even think." She was doing that to me one day in my mother's house, and followed me to the bedroom. I felt trapped! Couldn't get away from her! But she's got me really crazy, so I got all tensed up and with one blow—I'd been studying karate —one shot in the nose and it folded right into her cheek. I thought, "My God, what have I done?" It was the first time I had ever hit her like that. But that nagging, it really got me crackers and I just popped her. Broke her nose and she didn't even realize it. She wasn't crying; she was walking, you know, in shock, relatively calm. And when she felt around it, the first thing that came out of her mouth was, "I'm going to be ugly." Above all things, it wasn't the pain, it was the vanity that came to her. To this day, I'm amazed at her reaction.

We got to a hospital and found a plastic surgeon. He turned out to be a sculptor—I guess that goes hand in hand, sculpture and plastic surgery. He asked Amy if she wanted xylocaine or cocaine and before she could answer, he says, "Never mind." Because he knew which she would prefer by looking at both of us. He gave her cocaine and proceeded to take her to a room where he busted her nose more so as to reshape it and packed it up with cotton wads. I was in the waiting room and when Amy came out she was grinning. It's so funny because a little bit before she was panic-stricken and now she's stoned out of her mind because of the cocaine. So we went home and we were being nice to each other again.

I don't think she deserved to get her nose broken, but I don't feel bad about it either. I don't think I did anything particularly bad. You see, ultimately there is no right or wrong way. There are only things that are desirable and undesirable. I feel bad every time she throws that experience in my face. But it bothers me that she should harbor that and that she should be using that over and over again. And actually her nose is a little straighter than it was before.

Around that time we were trying to negotiate with the probation officer to go to New York City because we hear that probation is a lot easier there. People aren't on your ass all the time. And then along came an opportunity to save plane fare, a free trip, so Amy and the baby went ahead and

I stayed in Florida to save enough money to get our own apartment in Brooklyn. I got a job on a road gang, payloaders and tamping machines and setting up forms for the concrete for the edges of sidewalks. Little high school girls would stop to talk to the guys on the road gang. I'm all suntanned, kind of long-haired and muscular and just looking beautiful. One little girl caught my interest and I started fooling around with her. She was a virgin and wasn't ready to get laid, but she kind of got me excited and for the first time I started fooling around with someone. Then a couple of weeks later I met another girl and we got the thing off—a nice girl, wasn't crazy about it. She was a little frigid, actually.

While I was still in Florida, Baba died. He died on Amy's birthday. I went to the Baba house down there, you know, for both of us, and I was crying and some of the Baba people said, "Yeah, you feel pretty heavy, but dig it, man, you're not crying because of him. You're being selfish. You're crying because you lost somebody." As soon as they said that, I dug myself—that was just why I was crying. Baba's not dead. Like he told the people about two weeks before he dropped his body, "Nothing is ever lost. It's always there."

I kept sending Amy money and dope—I was really missing her and Sasha—and finally we got to the point where we had enough money and she found an apartment. Some friends helped me on the plane, put all my leather tools and everything aboard, and I flew into New York, where there's a blizzard going on. People couldn't meet me at the plane so I catch a subway with my baggage, get off according to directions in the neighborhood of this apartment. I've never been to Brooklyn before. I have no idea where I am. I come up at the Carroll Street exit and there's not a soul in the street. Snow's all over the place. It's very quiet, beautiful. I'm trudging through the snow, walking this way and the other, and then there's this one lonely little candle burning in a window. It's like a real Christmas setting. The minute I see the candle, I think, "This must be the place!" The warmth, the love, just were emanating from the window. I went up to the door, and sure enough, she'd printed a little sign, "The Cortazars." Amy was hugs and kisses. It was nice coming home. The baby was asleep and she'd prepared something to eat. Right away we take some mescaline to kind of get into the house and the energy and the spirit of us coming together and being a unit. The first christening of it.

Now begins the period of the Big Black Hole. You know, if you put yourself in a desirable growing environment, with two people having this intrinsic exchange of energy, you help each other to grow. You heal each other and become healthy. It's like putting a plant in ideal soil, giving it the right light, the right latitudes, the right air and moisture. Sexuality can even be eliminated from the process as long as you have that same intensity and understanding as you had when you were a child, as long as you both can still appreciate, for example, sitting in one spot and watching little ants walking around.

But if all those faculties don't complement each other and the environment is an ugly one and doesn't allow growth, you get sick. And you get sicker and sicker and sicker and that's what was happening to us both. We were finding an imbalance in our life, we were losing faith, and we were cussing out Baba—everything was in its most black kind of state. I was under pressure all the time, working ridiculous hours for an industrial cleaning company, busting my balls picking up all this dirty stuff that people had been trampling on all day. I was nervous at home and the pollution wasn't agreeing with me. And fighting, more fighting. A constant state of depression. The whole sexual activity is just disgusting. I mean it's like just making love to her to get off and she's just kind of laying there and trying to make good of it, but it's not coming across that way. And then

Sasha was starting to die on us with a blood disease he had started to develop. And the question was, "Why are we even living?" We were close to a state of suicide. Total loss of faith. And we are saying, "Our baby is going to die. What have we done? You goddamned fucking Baba, you no-good Baba. There is no Baba, there is no meaning to Baba."

Finally, Sasha came through and we had to take care of him and right about then I got sick, intensely sick, and went through three doctors and antibiotics, but nothing would help. Then some friends who go to Tai-Chi suggested Professor Chan Man-ching, physician to Madame Chiang Kai-shek. He's a Chinese herbal doctor and acupuncturist. Through a very complicated system of Chinese palpations, he diagnosed what I had through an interpreter. He told me that it was something very unusual, but that he could treat it. He wrote me out a prescription to be filled at a Chinese drugstore, prepared in a certain way. I had been bedridden for a month and a half, but over a matter of hours I was suddenly full of energy and ready to go to work. It's incredible. A small miracle had been worked.

That's when Amy and I started doing Tai-Chi-Chuan, which is training in sensitivity to the relationship of opposites. While studying this relationship of opposites, you are acting them out, very much like some type of therapy dancing. And sure enough, both Amy and I were becoming calmer, more balanced, and, Oh, there was a radical turning around in our consciousness. Our physical vehicle was ridding itself of its ailments and there were fewer distractions to our mental processes. We found a more balanced way of approaching sexuality too. We were sleeping with other couples. A new experiment in our life. We had found our faith again, together, slowly but surely. And something that had been plaguing me all my life, my allergies, were disappearing.

We had been in the city for almost a year and a half now

and we were dying to get out of it. Finally I got a chance to go up to the mountains to teach a leather class. It was really nice. I was featured in the *Village Voice* in an advertisement for this resort. Amy and the baby came along. It was such a good hit we decided to stay. We managed to rent a place from a chiropractor who was further help healing us, all this tension in our backs and all this distortion in our spines. So little by little we have come out of the Black Hole into a whole new Amy and Cesar, whole new people. We're in a healing atmosphere. We're even making love better now, getting closer again, and we decide one day we wanted another baby. So we plugged away and made a hit. When Amy was in the hospital having Krishna, a girl came to help until my mother could come, and being a young girl, we get it on and that wasn't objectionable to Amy. She's being very tolerant. We both visit her after she had the baby—it was a Caesarean, a serious operation, you know—but the girl liked Amy a lot as a friend so she felt we should tell her we had had a relationship. She wouldn't like to do anything behind her back. And Amy said, "Yeah, I figured you would." So that is how the experience was treated.

In the past, Amy told me that someday I was going to meet someone older, groovier than her. And I'd leave Amy for her. Mara might have been the woman of Amy's fantasies. Mara was forty-five and she's really been around, attractive, and she has a lot of things going for her. She is also a practitioner of Tai-Chi-Chuan, a little light in some ways, she's in the clouds sometimes, and other times she's so down-to-earth it's amazing. I had been digging her a long ways off, really attracted to her, and I didn't know that she was attracted to me. One day we were next to each other in a living room after a Tai-Chi dinner and I decided to be bold and touch her. She kind of leaned over me and then I started kissing her and she said something like, "You really light fires," which gave me an indication that she was really turned on. Then we assumed the Buddhist posture for joining male and female energy at a very high place. We sat in this posture where she crossed over in a half-lotus and I hold her and I was getting off. I was really reaching for very high levels of sexuality. We were both fully clothed; we were just really both there. I hadn't felt this good in I don't know how long. I had been making love to people, but this was really special. It proved to be the best hit I ever had.

So this began my next period of growth. I loved Mara, I loved the children, I loved Amy, but Amy made it difficult for me to live with her. And Mara was healing my spirit. But it was because of my relationship with Mara that Amy and I split up. Or rather that's the reason why Amy threw me out of the house.

I don't think infidelity is the thing that broke us up. The things that nagged at our marriage and that probably did break us up were the trivial, day-to-day things. Isn't it funny that no matter how far we trek along, how sophisticated we become in our concepts, what proficient systems and structures we manage to evolve, and how many people we manage to influence—isn't it something that after all our achievements and our creativity, when we come home we manage to be driven up the wall by our wives?

Amy Phillips Cortazar has retained much of the fresh prettiness which made her a cheerleader in the upper-middle-class suburb where she grew up. She has short, dark hair, brown eyes, and a light, rosy complexion. She speaks in a low, gentle voice even when recalling dramatic and painful incidents in her life. Now twenty-seven, Amy lives in New Hope, Pennsylvania, with her two children, Sasha and Krishna.

AMY:
The condition in which I met him is really what's im-

portant. I was going straight after being strung out on drugs for a really long time. I had just gone to Florida to get myself back together. I was about twenty-one, and I was trying to stop thinking about finding "*the* guy," which I was really hung up on since I was fourteen years old. I'd been in a lot of scenes since I left home; prostitution-type scenes and heavy drug scenes. I was really ready to clean up. And then I met my first Master, my first Spiritual Master, in Florida, and I really got turned on to that part of myself.

His name is Meher Baba. He was a man but a different type of man. And I turned on spiritually and realized that my life was not only going to be goals which I had thought of before, such as material things, but also that there was more to be gotten. There was a whole inner world, so to speak. It was really an incredible experience, the first time in my life that I had gotten high on something real, something that was going on inside me. It was like cough syrup. It was what I needed. I had had too much of the other extreme.

In the course of all this I met Cesar. He was into Meher Baba too. He'd been to the Edgar Cayce Foundation. He was always supremely sensitive and he picked up a lot of these things by himself. So when we got together we were a spiritual couple.

I thought Cesar was an Indian Prince. Everybody says, "God. He's so good-looking." And he is. Physically he's incredibly beautiful. But that isn't what particularly attracted me to him. It was sort of his mysticism that attracted me. And he was really attracted to me for the same thing. With him I felt really open. Or so I thought.

This was in Miami. I went out to get a job one day and afterward I went over to a friend's house to turn on and Cesar was there. It was like immediate attraction. I even invited him over for dinner. I went home and went to sleep and he woke me up at about eight o'clock that evening saying, "Where's my dinner?" I said, "I don't know, but far out. I'm going to take a shower." So I started to take a shower and he made a really delicious dinner. I really liked him. I didn't even think about liking him, but it was just there. We were really close right away. And he didn't stay over. He was really shy. It was beautiful.

The next day a cop came to the door in the early evening and said, "Does anyone named Amy live here?"

"Yeah," I said, "that's me."

He said, "You'll have to come with me."

The guy I'd owed the money to at the hotel got nervous, I guess, and told the police that I hadn't paid the bill. So I spent three days in jail. It was really OK, though. Like I had this really mystical experience there. I was thinking, I wish I had a copy of *Metaphysical Meditations,* you know, and a guy ten minutes later comes over and gives me a copy of it. So it was really great. My life was filled with experiences like that at the time. And Cesar seemed like he had to be a part of this whole big thing in my life. Right? He found out I was in jail and he couldn't do anything 'cause he had no money, but afterward, when I came home, he came over and we just stayed together.

I felt that I was a completely different person with him. In a completely different world. I was feeling new, from a whole different place. But through my whole life, the male-female thing was really the clincher. In school, getting good grades and being a cheerleader just wasn't enough. I had both of those. But a guy, that was the score. And there he was. Cesar really loved me. He really felt special about me. He never felt that before. He still loves me. And that's why he wanted to be with me.

From the beginning we had differences. Big differences. Background differences. And also he's two and a half years younger than me. But he was very old for eighteen. People always think that he's older than me. But at the same time he still hadn't moved away from home yet, so this was a big step. I was like a woman of the world, I guess. I mean, I'd done all the silly things that he'd fantasized about. Like I was brought up to think that prostitution was really bad, but it was the first thing I did when I left home. I only did it a couple of times. That's the way I always was. The first thing that I would think of was the first thing I wanted to do. And Cesar was glad that I wasn't into it anymore, but he was glad that I'd had the experience.

Spiritually, we were together—in theory, concepts, and idealism. Meher Baba will always be in my life—sure. Because he taught me that we are all one, and there's no separating us. We are one whether we want to be or not. Cesar and I went to meetings all the time and I learned a lot from him. We talked about reincarnation, that we had probably been together in the past. Stuff like that. We never had any problems there and we were always accepted in those circles.

We didn't really have a place. We didn't have jobs. But we got some money together, somehow. I probably wired my mother for money. And then we were living in a little one-room studio. A really cute place. We were spending most of our time in bed anyway, so it didn't really matter. We never had a dumpy place. Even if we were really in horrible places, our place was never dumpy. That was important to both of us. And that was really a beautiful time. All I remember is mangos and making love and really nice things. Florida. Dolphins. Like I had these beautiful Indian wedding beads that I always wore. And I never wore shoes, because it was so beautiful. I was always tan and healthy and sort of just free. In a body sort of way, I was just feeling so good.

A lot of our relationship was not physical, though. I felt that we had this great thing to work out, this mystical union. For some reason we were together and I felt we had always been together. We always talked to each other like we knew each other, I don't even remember any come-on. There was no fakery. I stopped looking at other guys. This was it. This was what I had been waiting for.

He said, "Will you marry me?" and I said, "Yeah." I didn't know anything about marriage. We sort of said it'll make our parents happy. "We'll do what we want to do but we'll get married." His parents were really against it, because they knew he had been fickle in the past. They were afraid of it. And I called my mother to tell her and she said, "What college did he go to?" And I said, "He's eighteen."

It wasn't much of a wedding. His parents were there. They didn't even have a little party for us afterward. Instead, they gave us three days at the Cadillac Hotel in Miami. Which was ridiculous. There we were—hippies at a Miami hotel. We ate. We had fun. He spent all our money giving the waitress a dollar tip every time I ordered a Coke. It was really silly. When we went to our room, they had two single beds, and I looked around and said, "Is this the kind of bed you're gonna give us?" and the maid goes, "Why? You all just get married?" and I said, "Yes." And she said, "You all want a honeymoon bed." So we go down to dinner and we come back up and they put three double beds together. This gigantic bed. It was really cute. We stayed in bed a lot. And then we tried to get a car together to go North.

It's funny, but the minute I got married I fell into all the patterns of what I knew about marriage. I thought I'd be different. I'd taken drugs and LSD and I was so cool and I knew it wasn't going to be the same. But it was. Because I wanted part of it to be the same. When we went to the city, I was still into drugs, but when we came home, I did the dishes. Three years of being out in the streets wasn't going to change what my mother had drilled into me for eighteen years.

In New York I got strung out—really worse than him. Because it was like my third time. And he was able to get it together. I didn't know how. I always trusted him not to really do anything bad. Like I never thought he'd get into a really heavy heroin deal where he'd have to carry a gun. He's very honest and stuff. His soul is very sweet.

Being back in Florida was a really heavy scene. For some reason Cesar always had a hard time getting along with people. I was one of the first people that really loved him. I don't think he was loved too much before that. People have always loved me. I've just been lucky. No matter how fucked up I got, they always loved me. But he was not loved and he became jealous of that.

At one time, people accused him of being a narc. Everybody hated him. I mean, it got so ugly that one day we went to a love-in and at the love-in he got punched in the eye. Pretty heavy. There were times that I doubted him. Why *do* people think this? One day I asked him, "Are you?" And he broke down in tears, "Why do you think that of me?" Then he got real mad at me and said, "You don't love me." I was confused and it really hurt me. But I had to work it out with him, even if he did do it. Even if he had turned around to me one day and said, "I did turn somebody in," I would have stayed and comforted him. It wouldn't make any difference. I was really committed. I couldn't say, "It's getting a little heavy, so good-bye." I was married to him and I felt that this was something that we had to see through together.

We wanted to have a baby, but the problem was how to take care of it. I still wanted to do creative things and stuff. But the only way Cesar could survive with it was to do it very middle class. So I said, "Okay. However you can do it, it's okay with me." But that's where my conflicts started. I thought, There's nothing wrong with having a baby and loving somebody. But our life-style changed when Sasha was born. And that was very uncomfortable. We went shopping on a certain day. We did laundry on a certain day. I stopped drawing. He was a construction worker. It was the only way to make any money. He couldn't bring home $30 a week anymore in leather. He had to bring home $80 a week. But we were still hippies. Because the other—that's not what we *really* were.

We were the first ones to have a baby. We had a lot of single friends. I would get a little jealous sometimes of the girls. And I wasn't exactly Marilyn Monroe anymore. But I know he loved me. I never really thought he would want to be with someone else. Well, maybe I did. He would pass a woman and say, "Isn't she good-looking?" or "Doesn't she have a gorgeous pair of legs?" I didn't mind, though, because he felt that he should tell me rather than keep it to himself. So he'd tell me. But finally I would say, "Well, don't. I don't like it. I don't want to hear about it."

Sometimes he'd take out a *Playboy* and really get into it. Did you ever see someone on speed get into something? I'd get really mad because I thought it was degrading our sex, because it was really lustful what he was doing. It made our sex not special anymore. So I'd say, "I'm leaving you," and he'd hit me.

Before we went back to New York we stayed with his mother. He wasn't working. He'd go out and come back, but he never came home with a job. And then one evening we had this really big fight. It was just the same situation we'd been in so many times. I said, "I'm going to divorce you," and he said, "What?" I was sitting on the bed and he was standing in front of me. And I said, "I'm going to divorce you." Boom! He hit me. I fell back on the bed. And I remember my nose—it felt like rain and crackling. I got up and looked in the mirror and I couldn't believe it. I lay back down again, crying. And he was going, "Oh, no! I'm sorry. I didn't mean to do it!" And you know, I never held a grudge. It's not one of my traits. I knew he was sorry. And my getting mad wasn't going to help it. So I said, "It's all right. Don't worry." And then I looked in the mirror at my poor

nose. Would it ever go back? It was like on the side of my
face. By that time his parents are rushing toward the bedroom. And his mother gets a peek in the door and says to
her husband, "Her eye fell out." They were furious at Cesar.
But then they realized this was no time to get mad. I was
sitting there bleeding with a broken nose. And I defended
him to them. I said, "It's all right, Mom. He didn't mean to
do it." And she goes, "How could you be with him?" and I
said, " 'Cause I love him."

Maybe it was masochistic. I don't know. I don't put
labels. I just thought the bad things were something I had
to go through. It was part of my growth. My soul.

But that did it for me sexually with him. How did I
know that he wouldn't get mad at the way I was fucking and
strangle me? You can say, how come I was living with
somebody like this, but spiritually he was so sensitive. The
tender moments that he showed were so beautiful, they
overcame everything else. Look, it's easy to love somebody
who's always kind to you, who's always good to you, who is
always feeling good himself and makes you feel good. But I
don't know anybody like that. But it's not easy to love
somebody who's not perfect. Yet all the Masters in the
world say that's where it's at.

I felt that we were both very good-looking and spiritual
and that we knew a lot more than most people. And we
tried never to hurt people. We tried always to be fair. Cesar
might have beat me, but he was fair. Like I pushed him to it.
He's very smart. He can figure out anything he wants. I've
never seen him try to do anything that he couldn't do fairly
well. I'm not that way. I'm just interested in being with
people and learning that way. But the combination of us
was really good. A lot of people used to say they really loved
us. Together, we looked really great.

After we'd been in Brooklyn for a while there seemed to
be something wrong with Sasha. Whenever he knocked into

things he would be black and blue and red. So I took him to the doctor, and he took one look at him and he said, "Does anybody hit the baby?" I got really defensive. Luckily my mother was still alive. She was with me when we went to the doctor. Then two doctors came back in the room and one of them sat down really serious-looking. And I remember I wished that they'd disappear. And I said, "What's the matter?"

"Sit down," they said.

And I said, "I don't want to sit down. What is it?"

They said, "The baby doesn't have any platelets in his blood."

I said, "Could he die?"

And they said, "Yeah."

I felt like the first time I had gotten off on heroin and my knees were weak. I said, "I want to know what it is. Could it be leukemia?"

And they said, "Yeah."

My knees gave out and I just fell. I was wiped out. They said I'd have to bring him to the hospital for tests. But those were the times when I knew why Cesar and I were together. Because I wouldn't have been able to do it with anybody else. No one. Even if it was leukemia, we had faith in something so great that maybe we could survive it. We stayed up every night together and prayed constantly. The hospital people were very nice. I remember I gave Sasha my Meher Baba locket and put it in his room. And then about ten thirty the nurse came into his room and said, "It's not cancer." It was this other rare disease. They gave him cortisone. I stopped giving it to him after about eight months. The doctor said I was crazy but I just couldn't do it anymore. I've studied faith healing since and he's doing fine. He's doing a lot better.

We moved to New Hope and we spent a lot of time together. We were always growing and learning about other

people. We learned about music together. We studied
martial arts together. Spiritually we shared a lot. We shared
a lot of everything except sex. In the beginning, sex had
been great. I was the young girl. But once I became his wife
and the mother of his child, he could no longer feel passionate toward me. No one else had ever had any com-
plaints about me, but he did. With Cesar it was so conscious. "Should I touch him?" or "I wish he'd do this to me."
I like to feel something before I even touch somebody.

We didn't really talk about it. He didn't like to talk.
Except when he was angry. He'd say, "Don't pull my hair
like that," or "When you kiss like that it turns me off," or "I
love when your ass feels like a young girl's ass." I felt Cesar
wanted my ass tighter and I didn't know how to do it. After
he said things like that I always felt, "What am I doing
here?" It was a drag, a big drag. I'd say, "Get the fuck away
from me," and I'd get out of bed. I'd say, "Man, I'd rather
sleep with a hat and coat." And he'd say I'm frigid and I'd
say finally, "You're right." I copped out with, "I guess I'm
just not sexual." And I thought there must be something
seriously wrong with me, cancer or something.

He was sleeping with other people and he'd say, why
don't I do it? Why don't I go out and meet guys? And I'd
mumble, "I don't know." One time we made love with this
couple and it was all right. I had a good time. I'm a person.
But he said, "Aha! You *do* like it." And I didn't really want
to. And that's when I started to see my friend, my Teacher,
in the city. He has this martial arts school and I didn't think
Tai-Chi was doing for me what I wanted. It deals so heavily
with the spirit and I felt that the thing that I studied should
be in accordance with nature. When I went there the first
question I said to him was, "I think I'm really sick. I don't
want to fuck everybody. It feels disgusting to me." And he
said, "What are you— a cat or a dog? Of course you don't."
And at that moment I just knew that I was right.

So for a long time there was no sex between Cesar and

me. I got used to him sleeping around. I mean, there wasn't any *one* person, but it was inevitable that something would happen. And then, after Krishna was born, it happened.

Mara is forty-six and Cesar liked the way she fucked. Yes, he loved this woman sexually—and it's such a strong force. I can really understand it—after so many years of not having it. I had not been sure that sex was that important. I thought, If you're going to live with a person all your life, maybe there's a year you don't fuck. But after so many years of not really having it, finally experiencing it again and saying, "I want this!" I can understand that. But Cesar didn't really know what to do, because he did love the kids and he did love me. We'd been together a long time. Like brother and sister. We really were one, probably more one than any other couple I know. He said he wanted both Mara and me, and I said, "You've never been able to support me." Not that there's anything wrong with it. If he could have handled it, I'd have said, "Fine."

Then he said, "I just feel like going to the desert for a year."

"Go," I said.

"How can I go?" he said. "How will you live?"

"Go," I said. "Like, just go. I can take care of myself. Whatever is real will be real when you come back. I'll be here." And what he did instead, he chose to be here and live with another woman. I mean, he gave it all up for a really material thing—which is her.

I guess I know what I want now and I already have it with one person. My Master. My friend. My Cosmic Lover. He teaches Tai-Chi. He makes me feel that I am beautiful and he wouldn't make me change for anything. When I'm with him, it's real. But I wouldn't live with him. I wouldn't live with anybody right now. As soon as you move in, the divorce starts.

JEFF AND NORA

Chronology

New Year's Eve, 1964	Jeff and Nora meet.
September, 1964–May, 1965	Nora is at Ohio Wesleyan; Jeff is at the University of Chicago.
June–September, 1965	Jeff and Nora live together in Chicago.
September, 1965	Nora enters the University of Chicago; Jeff enters Northwestern Law School.
February, 1965	They marry.
June, 1968	Nora graduates from the University of Chicago; Jeff graduates from law school.
September, 1968	Nora enters graduate school; Jeff begins teaching on the near West Side.
June, 1970	Nora leaves for Europe.
July–August, 1970	They travel together in Europe; the car accident.
September, 1970	Jeff takes a position as college dean.
April, 1970	The ménage à trois with Faith.
June, 1971	Their second European trip together.
December, 1971	Nora takes her own apartment.

6

The
Soul Mates

One of the most beautiful love myths is that of the Soul Mates. These lovers consider themselves the unique and perfect completion of one another, the sharers of an intense spiritual and intellectual intimacy. They know more about each other's tastes, thoughts, moods, and minds than any other person could possibly know. Together, they become one person. For them to have actually found each other is considered very rare indeed. And for them to marry is the stuff of fairy tales.

Jeff Miller and Nora Edwards believed in the love of Soul Mates and believed they found it with each other.

Jeff Miller is a lanky, good-looking man with a dramatic mustache and a sensitive and intelligent face. His manner bounces freely from the straight academic to the hip romantic. At the age of six months, he was adopted by a working-class family in Chicago, where he grew up. Presently, he is an assistant dean at the University of Chicago and the author of several articles on law.

JEFF:
I am sitting here six months from my thirtieth birthday, and when I think back, it does come close to love at first

sight. "Some Enchanted Evening Across a Crowded Room"—that was really the way it was. Nora was seventeen and I was nineteen. I have a memory which to this day can bring tears to my eyes, of the first time I saw Nora. She was in a very chic little red dress, just turning around and looking over her shoulder at me. I was just—bingo!

We sort of played around with flirtations with each other. I'm always very strategic. In all my life I've never been turned down by a woman because I never ask until I'm certain that the answer's going to be yes. So I lay back, sending out my friend for scouting reports and scarcely more than a month later on Ground Hog Day you should see the likes of me going to a Sweet Sixteen party to meet her again. I took her home and that Sunday we just walked around Chicago, Lakeshore Park, the Art Institute, and really began to like each other.

By April—spring does things to me—I really think we fell in love. We realized that we were interested in being as close as possible to each other indefinitely and that we were doing a lot for each other.

From the start, there was a tremendous amount of talking—we'd go to films and plays. You know, there are people who somehow have a natural spiritual kinship and it is true that Nora and I have had that and still have that in a way I think I have not had and never will have again with any other human being. We were soul mates. So many people felt that we really were perfect for each other.

Also, the relationship was solidly sexual in ways that sometimes got wonderfully comic, like a Woody Allen movie or something. Like being naked in her parents' living room and having her mother get up in the middle of the night, come into the room, and say, "What are you doing?" Lights off, and we'd say, "Oh, just talking." That wonderful teenage furtive kind of sexual relationship. There's really nothing like it. Eventually I was run out of the house, finally getting caught in the act, with the door locked by her parents. Banned from the house for being a sexual pervert. But to this day I am rather proud of the balls involved in that sort of thing.

At the end of the summer, about a week before she left for Ohio Wesleyan, I realized that she was really going to leave and when I realized that—I remember these feelings very well—it was with a tragic depth that I feel only in contemplating my own mortality. Waiting for the "chair." In seven days Nora was going away to college and this relationship, this sense of at last having a place in the world, of having a family, was going to be over.

Those weekends at Ohio Wesleyan were unbelievable. Just living out a month in two days. We would do so much, live so much, that it seemed like an eternity. We would have sex until we were both physically dysfunctioned. My dick would cough and sputter instead of, you know—which in those days required some effort (*laughs*).

That year was really the confirmation of the strength of our relationship, that it held together through that trial by ordeal. It all worked out. The day of my college graduation was the day Nora returned to Chicago, for us to be together for good.

That summer we lived in a big apartment full of kids on Stony Island Avenue. It's funny how many details one remembers, like from the dormitories hearing the kids sing the Pet Clark song, "Downtown." I remember "Hang on Sloopy" was big that summer. All the windows open, "Hang on Sloopy," and one day somebody throwing a banana peel in our window. They were times when personal styles were really changing. In my college class, people walked in like Pat Boone and walked out looking like freaks. It was a very happy time, living together, smoking banana peels—that was what you did in those days—and playing strip poker with two of our neighbors, that sort of playful, very happy attitude toward sex and sexuality, just being very romantic.

We got married for one reason—Nora had a trust fund and if her parents approved of our relationship it would provide money for her. And since we assumed at this point that we were going to get married anyway someday—what the hell? Just one day we said to ourselves, Why don't we see what apartments are available? We went and found one and said, "Gee, it's nice. Why don't we move in?" We asked the guy when is it available and he said March 1 and we said, "Well, okay, why don't we get married?"

It was a major concession for me to agree to be married by a minister. We went to talk to him in advance, and before I could tell him that I didn't believe, he looked at us and said, "Look, I'm going to use some words in this service, like 'God,' and remember that they were always meant to be poetic and not meant to be taken literally." He undercut my whole act!

I really was digging the casualness of getting married. I had our wedding rings in my pocket and I came there by myself. I stopped off in Marshall Field's on the way to buy some cigars and I ran into an old girl friend of mine. She said, "What are you doing?" And I said, "Oh, I'm going to get married in about half an hour." "Aw, you're bullshitting me." And I pulled out the rings, you know. I loved it.

I'm sure we both had a very hard time keeping a straight face, this was such manifest horseshit, totally irrelevant to what we were about—standing up in front of this guy, saying a few magic words. That wasn't the thing which was spiritually uniting us! That wasn't the thing which was holding us together! We were united by something far stronger, far more essential than that. So that the wedding meant nothing. Then we went home and had a party with our friends in the apartment, just a typical party, and started living our life . . . I get a little fuzzy after that (*laughs*).

Nora once came up with the phrase that she was my "only living relative." Which really was true. You see, we were a team and we would thrive on the fact that between us we knew everything. Like when we saw architecture, I could tell Nora a lot about architecture. Or when I read a poem, she could tell me a great deal about that poem. That seemed the proper division of labor. Because we were one thing, one personality.

When I was finishing law school, I began to be incredibly hassled by the draft, and Nora was my only source of personal strength. The world was crumbling; everything was corrupt and rotten, and that drew us more in on each other.

I was very paranoid; I didn't know if I would have to leave the country or what. Nora wrote a poem about my nightmares about the war. I liked the poem, but what I didn't know was that she wrote an introduction to it, explaining my plans for draft resistance. The first thing I knew it was in print in the university newspaper. I was livid, really went temporarily nuts, because I was convinced that her revealing my plans in a campus newspaper would make the Selective Service System instantly pull my file. I felt it showed a fundamental lack of respect for my integrity on Nora's part. You see, the intimacy which gave her my every thought and my dreams and my weaknesses gave her the ability to use it against me. It's kind of like having a leak in your head.

But look, Nora is somebody I respect. Maybe she was right. One of her jobs in our "corporate self" was to be direct, to get me away from the defended, the secret, to open up. I felt that I was too socially closed. But the fact is that I was the one who could have spent two years in jail, not Nora.

We were "soul mates," but I think that when a relationship emphasizes the spiritual and the intellectual so much, as ours did, it downplays the sexual. If we had a choice between talking and fucking, we would talk. And it seemed like the height of humanity to have reached that point. But sex is terribly important. I think that Nora's

thought at the start of our marriage was that our relationship was more important than her sexual playfulness, so she will give that up. But she has an essential nymphomaniac streak that always gave me great anxiety. I wouldn't dance with her in public because of the way she played up sexually to other people. Somehow it was inappropriate to relate to other men not only sexually, but more sexually than to me. You know, she wanted all of them to want her and half of them to try. Put that against my personality, the "motherless child" who wanted security and a family, and you see a real problem.

There eventually began a cycle of her nonresponsiveness to me, of relative frigidity. She began to develop rituals of foreplay that involved her being stimulated by my hands and fingers and, well, they might as well be her hands and fingers. I mean, it was so prolonged that it bordered on masturbation. It seemed to me that her sexual tastes drifted toward that and it made me feel as though I were a failure sexually, if all she needed me for was to masturbate her.

I consider myself completely uninhibited sexually and always have, but I blamed myself for her nonresponse. I felt then that if a woman doesn't respond to me, it is my fault, because I am in control of the whole act, that sex is something a man does to a woman, and that if she is not screaming in ecstasy I'm just not doing it right. And as a result of that kind of thinking, you don't do it right!

Just talking about this, I can feel that anger again. I remember those years of diminished self-esteem, the years of thinking of myself as incompetent. And the exhilaration when I finally did break out of that—I'm a real man after all!

By the spring of 1970, the party was over as far as the way we lived. I was about to take a real job—we had lived together as students first, then to get out of the draft I went to be a schoolteacher on the West Side. Here I was, the long-haired, hippie-dippie teacher with the slum kids. It was a very attractive, freewheeling, fun kind of life-style for us, having tons of time together, loads of things to do. But we both sort of saw a period of our lives ending and Nora, I think, was feeling crowded by a different life up ahead. I started looking at jobs at the university. One day we were riding on the Midway bus passing the college on the way down to vote. Somehow at that time it struck Nora that I was actually planning to lead a regular life. She saw me really getting on the conveyor belt, about to step into a conventional life and become one of *them* and no longer one of *us*, and she started crying on the bus. I found this outrageous because here I was overjoyed that I had a chance for these jobs. I can barely explain it—it was as though she had learned I was a war criminal or something.

But it had always been clear in my mind that I was headed for some essentially mainstream thing, some regular job in the sense that you got up in the morning to do something and lived according to time schedules. But Nora —now this used to drive her crazy—if she came into the office when I started the job and I couldn't just stop what I was doing and go out for a walk with her, I was some kind of reprehensibly structured, miserable person.

In some respects we were casualties of the Women's Movement. Nora was captured by some of the ideological things, that if marriage is the sexual enslavement of women, then women must declare their independence. But I can't think of a person who was more of an ideological ally of the Women's Movement in those early days than I was. I was generally their lawyer on their picket lines. I negotiated with the Chicago *Trib* on behalf of NOW. But I think maybe Nora resented my Pygmalion style. I mean she always brought up about how I strong-armed her away from being a creative artist and toward being something more settled, professional—which I definitely did. But metaphors get mixed. The point is that she would almost deliberately not do things that she wanted to do because I wanted her to do those things.

That summer, we were going to go to Europe for the first time and because Nora got off from her job a month earlier than I did she decided to go to Europe ahead of me. I couldn't believe that Nora would want to do that in the context of how much it meant to us to discover things together. But when I said that, she considered it a classic version of my stifling enslavement—what was I going to get by depriving her of something? She was going to show that she could live alone for a month, travel in Europe and take care of herself. But I did have the sense that if Nora went away to Europe for a month, there was no way she wasn't going to have a guy in every port. And I knew it with such certainty that under seventy-two hours after she left, I met someone and slept with her.

On the plane over, I was bullshitting with the guy sitting next to me. I was saying, "Well, my wife has been in Europe for a month and I've been back in Chicago," you know, I was really putting on the number, Joe Cool. You see, there was a lot of jiving of myself at that point because I didn't know if she beat me to it or not. So I came over on this plane bullshitting this guy about how cool it all is: Look, he's got to break out of his bourgeois monogamy, to start living and expressing himself and getting in touch with his feelings, you know. But it was so much horseshit. When I saw Nora, she instantly had to confess to me that she had had an affair with a guy in England, and she obviously had had a good sexual relationship with him. And she had met other men. I went into paroxysms of anger, jealousy.

What she had done was clearly different from what I had done because I had been acting in self-defense. Nora was the operator and I was the reactor. That day in Zurich, I was horrendously hostile to Nora, yelling at her. It was touch and go whether we would split up at that point, but we decided to rent a car and try to work things out. Still, I was really hostile. I used words to the effect that she was some kind of fucked-up, debased person who needed to do these things for sick reasons. The hostility and venom were severe to the point of physical violence, like grabbing her arm very hard while she was driving.

And yet it's really amazing that in spite of all this, we had a wonderful time in Switzerland. It was the reassertion of the idea that between us we could take care of anything. We would just storm a town and she would meet somebody who could introduce us to somebody. She would just incredibly line things up and I would instantly learn how to fake the language, whatever it was. I think the reassertion of what we had as a team pulled us through another year. It still was clear how much strength we had together, functioning, enjoying things, and how much that overpowered, or at least counterbalanced, tremendous pain.

I was very turned off sexually the first three or four days. But by the time we reached St. Moritz, I was feeling romantic again and one night in a lovely old town called Zooz we had sex for the first time again and it was good. It seemed that I could almost convince myself that this whole business had been rejuvenating. You see, I never questioned that Nora's deepest affinities were with me, her unquestioned love was for me, that she had no emotional stake in those other men.

But then while we were in Paris—Nora was using a diaphragm at that point—she ran out of the shit that you put in the diaphragm. She had used it all up in the month before me, and moreover, could not locate the stuff in Paris! Again, I felt betrayed. She had clearly chosen: Well, I got two tubes and I'll leave a quarter for Jeff. Shit. Here I was beginning to trust her sexually again, you know, putting it behind me. But it turned out to be a convenient out for both of us not to have sex for the rest of the summer. It took the heat off.

Something significant happened in France. I still don't
understand it. Around Bastille Day, I decided we would go
to Mont-Saint-Michel and Chartres. So we drove and on the
way back we were coming from Mont-Saint-Michel and we
were in a severe car accident while Nora was driving. To this
day I honestly don't know if she was trying to kill me! The
fact is that my half of the car was plowed into a concrete
post at sixty miles per hour and I spent a couple of days in
the hospital in Normandy. Again there was a lot of hostility
and nervousness and anguish in the air. It was classic Nora:
not knowing how to drive, just got a driver's license, and
whipping down the roads in France, going around a turn
way too fast, losing control of the car and hitting the accelerator instead of the brake. Like sex, here was just another example of where the Nora life-style was leading to
ruin.

But there were still good times despite the sexual thing.
It somehow didn't seem so odd during the summer, the
absence of sex. I think from that point on we just sort of
gave up on each other sexually—we decided we would find
others.

By the fall of 1970, we were definitely moving in the
direction of sexual openness in front of each other. Maybe
that would have been the way out, by the way. If the two of
us had met a couple, we might have been able to pull it off.
Because if you are doing it in front of each other, then you
are *doing it together*.

Faith started out as Nora's intellectual protégée—this is
a heavy story—but we sort of came to like each other, me
and Faith. I think she was taken with my rugged good looks
(laughs). I felt that she was a pretty sexy little girl. Good
thin body! So, Faith broke up with her boyfriend somewhere along in the year and had no place to live. Well, why
didn't Faith come to live with us for a while? We could put
her up on the couch. One night as fate would have it, we

were up late talking and we thought, what was the sense of Faith talking over all that distance? Why didn't she just come in bed with us? Nora and Faith were great political activists and determined that the dictates of sisterhood included a willingness to yield up possessiveness of one's husband. So Nora had given Faith the green light. We sort of were falling asleep together and I had my arm around both of them because they are, after all, my pals! (laughs). And Nora said, "Would you two like to be alone?" And, why not? At this point, I think Faith had her hand on my joint. (I'm being glib, this is actually very serious stuff.) Nora went into the next half-room, really behind the bookcase, to feign going to sleep while Faith spent the better part of the night doing real "deviated perversions" (laughs).

My mind was divided. I thought it was neat that we were all having this wonderful open relationship. And for a while we really sustained this fantasy that Faith was in love with me and we could have an affair while all three of us lived together. I was also thinking that this was a good fucking lesson for Nora. I cared deeply for Nora, but I felt in control. Nora started getting very unhappy because I was spending, just for the sheer variety of it, more time with Faith than with her. I remember walks with Nora when she was crying and she understood that she had worked out a way of punishing herself.

Then it was time to go to Europe again, and time for Nora to go before me. I joined her two weeks later and again we had a fantastic time traveling. Though my relationship with her was still pretty sexually messed up, it still had enough strength, enough importance, enough beauty —again, that kinship—that it just wasn't worth being involved with Faith and so when I came back I ended that.

You see, I still preserved the idea of the specialness of my relationship with Nora. I felt that *we are each other's people.* That no matter what else—the suffering—Nora was my person: Whatever she was doing, we would find a way. That was part of our dialectic. We would fight like crazy and be back again, you know, a day later. I remember that a colleague of mine used to compare his relationship with his wife, which was obviously falling apart at the seams, with mine and Nora's, and I used to say to myself, "Where does this schmuck get off comparing these people who don't belong together, who are acting hostilely to each other, to me and Nora, who are each other's people?" We were a superior relationship. We were really up front. If Nora felt like doing something, she did it, and if I felt like doing something, I did it. It seemed ludicrous that people could suggest that this had something to do with the relationship collapsing.

Somehow there was a renaissance of interest and loyalty in that period right after we returned from Europe. That's August, but by December Nora and I were apart, never to live together again to this day.

Nora once again started talking more and more about independence, about, oh, she should be free to go to Europe for a year if she wanted to, that she should probably have her own apartment. We fought, wept, at one point I crumpled up our marriage license and threw it at her. She was doing everything to be independent of me. Like even though my income at that point was twice hers, every bill had to be split fifty-fifty at her insistence, so that she wouldn't depend on me, so she could develop the discipline to be independent of me, so that she could split at any time. I guess that all said to me, I better dump before I get dumped.

I really made the punishment fit the crime. I met a beautiful girl who was separated from her husband and we decided to comfort one another. The relationship was like heroin. I became addicted to it. It was threatening to Nora in every possible way, a slender, perfect body at a time when

Nora's body wasn't, a really sexually exhilarating experience at a time when Nora had none. I said, "Look, Nora, I understand what you've been talking about all these years. Our relationship is terrific, but it can't provide me with everything. You give me everything I need except sex and Ann gives me all the sex I could possibly dream of. And I like it the way it works."

I really was schizophrenic. I was living two lives in two different ways and I was at peace in both of them. I would go off with Nora for a few days and have a terrific time in her Nora-ness and then four days with Ann and I was in sexual ecstasy and I never dropped a stitch in my work. By December—by which time I wasn't coming home every night—Nora said she couldn't stand it and would just have to get out. She found her own apartment, but the idea was still that we would be together with two apartments, with both of them as our homes. I thought that would be a nifty idea for a marriage, to be together when we chose to and be separate when we chose to—an ideal marriage.

But in fact we weren't together from then on. The times when we would be together dropped off radically, till by the spring I was living with Ann. But it wasn't until the fall, when I met Sandy, that I really realized that I could have an integrated relationship with someone else, you know, both sexual and intellectual, and without the sick history I had with Nora. Only then could I really begin to let go of her.

In lots and lots of profound and basic ways I remain very close to Nora. It makes as much sense for me to deny my relationship to her, my need for her, as it does to deny a relationship with a relative, with a parent or a brother or a sister. You know, when people are fundamentally linked, they can't create the fiction that they aren't. That's sort of the way I feel sometimes, even to the extent of major fantasies, like why couldn't Nora and I go through life as each other's adopted sister and brother?

Dark-eyed and delicate-featured, Nora Edwards Miller is alternately intense and bubbly, but there is a directness that pervades all of her moods. She grew up in a wealthy suburb of Chicago, where she attended private schools. She is a magna cum laude graduate of the University of Chicago. Currently she is completing her PhD dissertation in literature there, while working as a waitress in a feminist restaurant in Hyde Park. She is a poet and essayist whose work has appeared in several magazines.

NORA:

Oh, Jesus, this is going to be hard *(laughs)*. I'm not up to this. I haven't been through analysis yet, you see *(laughs)*.

Jeff and I met at a party when I was seventeen years old. He was the friend of the brother of a friend of my friend's girl friend. You know, one of those things. It was a New Year's Eve party and I guess Jeff just stood out. I remember he did drink a whole bottle of Grand Marnier—which I thought was very impressive.

I was not immediately attracted to him but I was very interested in him. I think it started out with me feeling he knew much more than me, that he was much smarter and might be a guide in life. He could help me develop, and I was very anxious for that.

As soon as I really began to look forward to seeing him, he slapped me across the face essentially by telling me that I was too young for him and he couldn't see me anymore. I was totally devastated! Then, about two weeks later, he came back from his Glee Club tour, called me from the terminal, and said, "I really want to see you." I mean, it was such a manipulative trip and I was such a stoop for it. I think he wanted to do a somewhat sadistic thing to me so that I would be put in my place early in the game. And I loved it *(laughs)*. How dare you do that to me? Do more! Yeah. So that's how it started—and that's how it ended. Do you need to know anything else?

It was spring—a perfect time for the blooming of love—and that other stuff just didn't matter. He was just too important and very soon we found ourselves saying to each other, "You are my whole life, you are my person, I finally found you and I'm going to keep you for the rest of my life."

I thought I was more myself with Jeff than with anybody. I still do, no question about that. The one very strong thing that kept Jeff and me together was that each of us saw the other in the best possible way that he or she could be seen. Suddenly you find someone who says, "You're really terrific. You really've got it."

I remember the first summer we spent together. I had just gotten out of high school and was living at home. I got different kinds of jobs in the city and I eventually wound up working in the bra and girdle department of Marshall Field's. It was very Sisyphusian. No matter how much you folded the stuff on the table, five minutes later some little fat woman would come and mess it all up. Jeff was working at his father's place and he would pick me up at Marshall Field's at six o'clock and we would just spend the entire night together and I would never come home. I would just touch base, change my clothes, and that would be it. We spent a lot of time in Hyde Park. We went to the movies all the time. We just walked around. It was very romantic.

The first time we fucked was a big bust. We'd been doing "everything-but" for months and months and months. To me, he was a veritable gold mine of sexual information, because I had none. But of course I was afraid. Not that I didn't trust Jeff, so much as things like parental disapproval or what happens if I get pregnant. That was the main fear.

Now, the first time I said yes, I put on this fantastic red dress. I was excited, anxious for it, I wanted it to happen. But I didn't know what it was going to be like. I didn't know if it was going to be that different from everything else we had done.

It was all very romantic. Except there was something vaguely comical about the whole thing because it was such a setup. Now we were going to do *it!* He naturally had taken care of the precautionary measures. He had procured a Jeff Miller super scum bag. Meaning, of course—the most expensive, bizarre, exotic thing he could get his hands on to impress me with. Just like the Grand Marnier. It turns out that it cost $1.50 for one and it came very heavily wrapped, like a Chinese box.

So we got into bed and the first thing I do is laugh! Very bad. Very wrong for the occasion. But that's because I was so nervous and the whole thing was so funny and Jeff was so stern and earnest about it. He was going to get that in, no matter what. So we did it and I don't remember it being at all a passionate thing. I was just trying to understand everything and look around and figure out: What's he doing? What's this? Hmm, that's not so bad. But he was into it, of course, and so he came and he burst the scum bag. Right through! And I knew that this was the punishment! Not only was it not so terrific and I didn't care one way or the other if we ever fucked again, but I was sure that I was going to be pregnant. My life would be over. I went into a hot bath and he sat me down and he gave me a Coca-Cola. Then I just went out to sit on the balcony and look at the river. I just sat there feeling terribly contemplative, sad, and tragic—just tragic.

When I went to Ohio Wesleyan, it was very hard for me to remain faithful to Jeff. Not that I thought there was anyone I would meet better than Jeff, but I was so lonely. And I was awfully alive at that point sexually. But as soon as Jeff came down there or I came home, everything we had between us was completely restored. We filled the moments with so much discussion and feeling and sharing and fucking. It was terrific. There was no doubt in my mind when I was with him that I loved him and I hoped it would always go on that way. It was like an island, finding him. And vice versa. We had total understanding and affection.

Yet, still I'd say to him that all I wanted to do was go out with some guys and you can go out with some women just to see what they're like. Here I am in college and I feel like I'm married. No, I don't think I'm going to meet anybody that's better than you or more important than you or anything. I just want to know what it's like to be with another man, other men, before I commit myself to you. But he couldn't have stood that. So finally I just said to myself, "Oh, Nora, you're never going to be satisfied so just forget it. Nobody's ever going to be as terrific as Jeff," which is true—for me, anyway. And once I made that choice, then marrying Jeff meant nothing to me.

The wedding changed nothing. I was so married to him by that time that how could I possibly be more married? And anyway, as soon as I was married, I pretended that I was *not* married. Like being called Mrs. Miller. I would say, "Who are they talking about?" I didn't have any real model for not changing my name but I just hated it. Jeff would tease me about it all the time.

Those first years of marriage were fun. We didn't have any money. We did crazy things. Whatever we did we shared it with each other. First he got this job at American Industrials. They adored Jeff and so they gave him anything he wanted, including an assistant which was me. I got to write movie reviews occasionally. I adored it.

We were in school too. I was very successful as a student and I had a lot of positive feedback outside and Jeff was very proud. We were growing and developing, deciding who we were. We were choosing tastes. We were being happy together. We had friends that we liked. We shared everything in our lives together—except our feelings *(laughs)*. The big one!

We were happy, but I resented feeling that I had to fuck Jeff and I couldn't fuck anyone else and I hadn't fucked anyone else. After a while I brought that resentment with me into bed and I was very cold to him sexually. Not all the time, but as time passed, often enough so that it was pretty much of a drag. I couldn't say, "Try to understand me, Jeff. Is there something we could do?" I mean, I think that the feelings of possessiveness that he needs to feel and the fear of being possessed that I have in my personality operated to make sex bad.

The only reason I went to graduate school was because Jeff had to be here for the draft. I remember everything now. It was just a series of crises! The draft made me feel the full extent of my moral degradation. Why, you ask? Because I was so torn by the feeling that I had to do something to help Jeff to get out of it. The only thing that I could do to help him would be to have a baby, and we would talk about it and he couldn't understand. I would have much rather have gone to Canada to live than have a baby. He really didn't want to do that. He just thought his whole life would be ruined.

He was, in some ways, a very selfish person. It's hard for me to say it because I so much believed that I was the one who was self-centered—and of course I am. But he made me feel that he was better and I was worser. I really thought that to have these thoughts, about the draft and having a baby, about sex with other people, confirmed a sort of moral shallowness in me—an essential baseness of some sort. I have struggled with those feelings for as long as I can remember. As a child, I would remember thinking, "Well, Nora, it's time to reform." And I would plan this regime of various things that were going to be reformed. And I never did any of them.

The Women's Movement gave me another place to form an identity. Before that it had only been Jeff. I felt disloyal, but it was terribly exciting at the same time because it was all very real and necessary. I have never understood how the Women's Movement brought us apart but in fact it did. I mean, I probably would have been the last person in the world to have gotten involved in it without Jeff. Jeff would come to the meetings! We couldn't be apart for five minutes. He was an ardent feminist and he would say that he believed in feminism well before any other man I had known would say it, but he acted as if he were a Victorian husband—which he was. He even looks like a Victorian husband.

So here we were in this spoken relationship where everything I wanted to do with my life—to lead it independently and discover an identity of my own—was all right. And yet any time anything like that actually happened—like when I went away to Europe by myself, or when I didn't want to use his last name, or when I wanted to experiment with separate bank accounts—it was utterly devastating. Those were incredibly painful things for Jeff and he took them very personally.

I guess the fact that he was becoming someone in the world outside of us made me uncomfortable too. I don't know what I wanted him to become, but when he told me he'd gotten a job as a Dean, I cried. He felt that it was such a symbol of my not wanting him to succeed—which it wasn't. It was a fear that I would be left out. That I would feel phony and be called upon to be a faculty wife. And I would have to meet people that I didn't respect and felt antagonistic toward because I had been a student and pretty involved in some ways with the '68 stuff. In fact, I didn't know what a Dean did. How the hell did I know what a Dean did? I never went to see a Dean in all my four years of college. But I thought it was bad. Because all we had been screaming for years was, "Kill the Dean!" I used to call him "The Pig." He didn't like that.

I don't think there's anything about Jeff and me, intrinsically, that would have made sex bad. For one thing, in the beginning, it was successful. Part of the excitement with Jeff came from the feeling that we had met our mate in life. And that never changed. Even now. But does that kind of love go with sex? Is sex a function of being involved with somebody who's very different rather than somebody who's very like me? I only know I never felt worse in bed with anyone in my life than I did with Jeff.

So I tried to have affairs. I wanted to leave Jeff and be able to come back to him. I just wanted to bring a little freedom to myself. But it was disastrous.

I had an affair with a guy in one of my graduate seminars. He was bisexual—probably much more gay than he was bisexual. But he excited me because he was, well, for one thing—available. And two—he was so completely eccentric and bizarre that it was a relief. This was the decadence that Jeff had long feared I would involve myself in. So I did—and it was such fun. And it didn't hurt anybody.

You have to understand that I never thought I didn't love Jeff. I never thought that we would be apart, in fact. I thought we were undergoing changes. The person I felt most real with and most alive with—I mean, it's like being high—was Jeff, and it still is. I almost feel this sort of transcendental thing—that there are just certain people, for whatever reason, who excite you in a way that other people don't. But what I didn't understand was that it's possible to love somebody that way and not want to be with them all the time. I felt so frustrated and claustrophobic at that point. That's when I went to Europe for the first time by myself and that was decisive—the end of a phase of the relationship—the beginning of the end.

Going off by myself was the proof that Jeff's worst fears—"I will leave you"—had been fulfilled. I left him. And yet I went away thinking that I was doing a perfectly innocent and nonhostile act. And as soon as I got there I had an affair with somebody. It was so obvious to everyone that I would, and I don't know why it wasn't more obvious to me.

Drake was even younger than I was and I was pretty young. And he picked me up. Yes. He picked me up in Trafalgar Square. I mean, it was just one of those things. I had come right off the plane. I saw him as dangerous and unknown. Really unsafe! Really unsavory! He was the most sexy, most adorable sweetheart I have ever known.

Of course I never let my mind conceive of a relationship with him. With Jeff the sexual excitement was, "This is the world in my arms." With Drake it was a much more limited thing. I wasn't feeling the world. I was feeling like a flower—that's all. Like something being reborn that was tired out and is now opened again.

When Jeff met me in Switzerland, I immediately told him that I had had an affair with a man in London. I'm not subtle. I've never been private. And I probably wanted to hurt him. I wanted to punish him for being weak. Because I thought his wanting me so desperately and fearing my leaving him meant that he was a weak person. So I told him and the expiation of this was unbelievable. We were driving a little Volkswagen on these mountain roads and he would suddenly get angry at me and pull the wheel out of my hands. It was really crazy stuff and I was terrified. But we also really had a good time and as soon as he got over the fact that he could never touch me again *(laughs)* we had terrific sex also.

He made me drive and I didn't know how to drive at all. I had gone for a driver's license before we came and I had only three lessons. I took the test and I passed and here I was with a car. He claimed I tried to kill him in the accident. Actually, he had much more intention of killing me every time he swerved the car.

We knew it was going to happen seconds before. And I think what happened was that in panic I put my foot on the accelerator when I meant to put it on the brake. We just charged into this railroad track cement thing. Luckily Jeff put his hand up so his whole arm was cut, but nothing else. All I remember was him saying to me, "Nora, you have to get me out of this. You have to help me. . . . You have to do it." And I said I would.

The whole time he was in the hospital I had to scout the streets finding things to amuse him. A deck of cards. A little chess game. Anything. We had a good time in the hospital *(laughs)*. Then we spent the rest of the time in France going to different places to have the stitches removed as they became ready. Finally, in the South of France, we had his elbow stitches removed. And he saved the bloody shirt to wave at me! Then he had the audacity to have somebody sew it for him. He wears it all the time.

That summer was very disastrous and yet we probably had the best times of our lives together. We had a good time that following year in New York too, but I think the pressures never really let up after that because of the fact that I had had an affair. He was just waiting for the time to fuck me over. And it happened to take another year. And then, there was Faith. And I thought I was buying my peace with Faith.

This is a very painful thing. I met Faith because she called me up on the phone that year early in the fall. She said, "I've just read your master's essay and I loved it!" My first fan! So I said, "Who are you? Get over here!" She told me something about herself and I said, "Look, some friends of mine are getting together a consciousness-raising group, would you like to come?" So she came and I liked her very much from the beginning. I thought she was incredibly interesting-looking, sensitive and articulate, very striking. And I met Roger, the guy she was living with—very, very handsome. Which was the only thing I cared about . . . such a superficial thing!

In the spring—we had become very close friends at that point—Faith decided she really wanted to leave Roger. When she did she had no place to go, so I invited her to come and stay with us. That was really it.

No sooner had she moved in when she started talking about the fact that she was very jealous. She kept saying she was very attracted to Jeff and I think she felt very sad one night and we invited her into the bed with us and before long—you know. She was sort of asking my permission and I gave it without consulting Jeff at all. Jeff was just there. He was certainly not attracted to Faith. But I didn't think that he would, as it were, throw her out of bed. And I put her in bed. I really was trying to buy off my past infidelities. And I was trying to get a little bit of a bank account for the future. But I had no idea I was going to feel as horrible as I felt.

They began making love to each other. I was sort of there and not there. I was observing it. The thing I remember most is watching Faith's hand go through Jeff's hair. I couldn't believe that anyone else could put her hand in his hair that way. It just made me sick. But I didn't do anything. I had no choice at that point.

I finally got out of the bed and I went and slept on the couch because I felt very uncomfortable. In the morning, he got up and came over to me. He was very spaced out, but loving and affirming. I expected that would be that, not that an affair would be waged.

Jeff would tell me, "Oh, don't worry, I just want the sex." And I'd say, "Why do you spend your time with her instead of being with me," and he'd say, "Well, I have to do that in order to have sex." He was very pragmatic. This was the beginning of my understanding that Jeff could say he loved me, just like I could say I loved him, and hurt me terribly. I finally felt, Well, if you love me, how can you do this to me? Which is what he had been saying to me for years.

And yet I take full responsibility for the whole insane thing. In my heart I knew I caused it. And I guess the affair with Faith wasn't satisfying to Jeff because I did set it up. What he really wanted was to go out and find a woman on his own. Which is what he did the following summer when we came back from Europe. Very quickly. By November he was already involved with somebody else.

And as soon as I found out about it, I got an apartment of my own. I simply left. I couldn't take it. He says that I was ready to go, that I was always talking about leaving, but I don't remember it that way. I remember just feeling so hurt and so rejected. I was thrown out. I still feel all the time, just about every day, the sense of being abandoned. And it's like a shock, all the time.

This relationship was so unbelievably intense that for six or seven years no one could really come between us. No woman and no man could really make an emotional impression on either of us. But when they did, we could not withstand it. One affair. Then another. We couldn't handle it. But who, of all people, could know that? I the least of all, because I lived in such a fantasy world. We were just too bound together. Our identities were so merged. I had no idea who I was outside of Jeff and I didn't know that was true of me until I was away from him and I saw how totally nothing I felt. I felt I was nothing without him.

He thinks he has the kind of relationship now, with Sandy, that will provide him with the happiness that security genuinely does bring him. But security alone doesn't bring the kind of happiness that sustains a life. I think he's crazy. I think he's fooling himself because anyone who could experience the things we did together can't live that way for very long. They might for a time, but eventually they'll feel this terrible regret.

I think I know one thing without any reservation, and that is that I love Jeff still. Enough time has elapsed, enough things have happened to still say that, and know that it's true. I don't know if I would die for Jeff, but something awfully close. And I don't know what I would feel if we were living together again and were domestic again and patterned. I don't know. It's the best feelings I'm talking about. It's like looking for a home. And that's what he was *(crying)*. What is he that's so important and so great? So what. So who cares. I can't for the life of me figure it out.

MICHELE AND MARC
Chronology

1959	Michele and Marc meet in high school.
1960-61	Michele is at junior college; Marc is at school and working.
1961-63	Michele moves to Boston and works on a daily newspaper.
1962	Marc is in Providence, Rhode Island. They meet again at a wedding in Maine.
1963	They are married and move to Bridgeport.
1964	Pierre is born.
1965	They go to Florida; Marc works as an umpire.
1966	Marc returns and they move into their first apartment in Boston.
1967	Leslie is born.
1967-72	Both are working and raising their children in Boston.
1972-73	They move to a small town on Massachusetts' North Shore and separate eight months later.

7

The Simple Nesters

Uncorrupted by the lusts, egotisms, and ideologies of the aspiring classes, the Simple Nesters content themselves with modest family goals—a little security, a little comfort. In many cases, they come from a small town and a humble religious background. More than anything, they want to provide family love for one another, to make a little nest. According to the myth, that is what marriage is really all about, what it was originally conceived for, what many have lost sight of. In a sense, no myth is more romantic today than this one.

Michele Gameau and Marc Bricmont lived on the same street in a small Maine town since they were children. They fell in love as teenagers and, from the beginning, shared the Simple Nesters dream.

Michele Bricmont is a tall, loose-limbed woman with an easy, warm smile. Everything about her is soft, earthy, and comfortable. At thirty-two, she is a lively talker and an infectious laugher. She was born and raised in Auburn, Maine, the eldest of four daughters in a French-Canadian family. Currently, she lives with her two children, Pierre, nine, and Leslie, seven, in a tiny, second-floor flat on Massachusetts' North Shore.

MICHELE:

Marc and I grew up in a small town in Maine, a mill town, with predominantly French-Canadian Catholics. I always thought it was ugly. And cold, cold in a lot of ways. There were factories, and shoe shops, and the mills, and a dirty river running right through the town. People had a hard time there, a very hard time. I did an awful lot of feeling sorry for myself growing up there.

We were sixteen when we met. It was the summer before our senior year in high school. One day I walked into this pizza place where everybody hung out and there was a whole bunch of guys sitting around. He was one of them. I'd seen him around actually but he was shorter than me so I wouldn't even look at him. I was this five-feet-nine giant, right? Anyway, we all started talking about the next dance coming up, which was one where the girls ask the boys. And so they said, "Hey, Michele, you going to the dance?"

I said, "Well, I would, but I don't know who in the world I'm going to ask."

"How about me?" one said.

"Oh, you're too short."

"How about me?" another said.

"No, you've got a girl friend already."

"How about me?" Marc said.

"You're too short," I said.

And he stood up and said, "No, I'm not." So we went to this dance together and we had a wonderful time. I immediately fell in love with him. With his presence. And his blue eyes. And his smile.

You've got to understand that I was French-Canadian and so was Marc. I spoke only French till I was five. We were inferior to the English-speaking people. Also, I was very Catholic. It wasn't a matter of being a believer or anything. It was a matter of being terrified. I used to think that every thought I had was bad. And sex? Forget it! I was terrified. Before Marc, I had a few boy friends. I'd go to the movies with a boy and he would put his arm around me and I would start sweating *(laughs)*. I don't know why, but with Marc it was different. He had something very warm. And gentle. I trusted him because I just knew he had the same feelings I had.

From that first date, we were together every single night forever and ever. My mother used to have to throw him out of the house. We would hang out on the porch and neck. It was very romantic and I was really in love with him except I wouldn't sleep with him, of course. And we didn't know how to deal with that. We used to break up all the time just from the tension, and then he'd go out drinking with the boys for some kind of release. And that's when all the girls would break up with all the boys *(laughs)*. And yet Marc and I really loved each other very much, so sooner or later we would get back together.

I hated my home. My father was a plumber, but there was no work in town so he used to work at the other end of the state. He'd be gone all week and come home weekends. I often wondered why he had ever gotten married and had children. He would rather go out and mow the lawn than hang out with any of us after he'd been gone all week. When I was a year old, he left for World War II. My mother told me that before he left they were very much in love. But he had other women over there and that was the end. He'd almost died too, but *that* was the big black thing! She never forgave him all these years. They've been together for thirty-three years now and she never forgave him. Never talked about it even. It was a cold house.

But Marc had it much worse than me—he had no house. He was brought up in an orphanage from the age of three to eleven. By Catholic nuns. He didn't get any love, really. Finally, when he was eleven, his mother remarried and took Marc and his brother out of the orphanage and tried to make some kind of family for everybody. But he wasn't happy. He poured it all out to me. You know. Tears and recurring nightmares from what it was like when he grew up. And I feel those things so intensely. When someone starts telling about things that happened in their childhood like that I just sit and cry. I couldn't help him with those things. I could just love him. We talked a lot about homes. We just knew the two of us could do it better.

Whenever we broke up, I was shattered, of course. I remember one time we had broken up—for the eighty-eighth time! *(laughs)*—I was upstairs in my room and I wouldn't talk to anybody. Michele was going through her thing again! But then Arlene Meaker called—she was a doctor's daughter—and she said her mother was actually going to drive all the girls to the high school basketball championships in Boston and we were going to spend the night in a hotel. A hotel! It was so exciting, I forgot about Marc and everything.

That trip was so wonderful. Just the girls! Arlene's mother gave us a pajama party with plenty of Coca-Cola and potato chips—she had some nice family there. And then it was the day before the last game. If we won, we'd be New England Champions. And then somebody said to me, "Guess who's here?" I couldn't believe it. I had finally done an independent thing and he comes up there to find me. He hitchhiked to Boston by himself in the middle of the night and found me. So off we went together for a walk around Boston.

We'd never done anything like that. We had milk and a doughnut somewhere. We were in love again. And I was already walking off the sidewalk at this point. It was a beautiful day. Being somewhere else, feeling grown-up in a real city. We went to the game that night. We were in the last row of the old Boston Garden. I could hardly see the team, let alone what was happening down there. And we're sitting in the back row and he's crying and he's telling me how much he loves me and he's sorry. And I think that my spirit left and flew to heaven! We just sat there beaming. "Of course," I said, "of course. I understand. Whatever you want. I love you. You want me, I'm yours."

That following year, I was at junior college in Spring-field, Massachusetts, and Marc remained in Auburn working as a grave digger. When I came home that following summer, things were very difficult between us. I was still kind of that sick, crazy in love with him that I was before. But it was difficult. I had gotten a job in a very fancy resort called Poland Springs. And Marc was still in Auburn, but he would never come to see me. I would call him and he'd say, "Look, Michele, it's too far and I don't have a car." And I'd say, "Twelve miles is too far, huh?"

Once I hung up the phone, crying, and I went back to work at my little job there. Afterward, we all went out to the bar across the street and there was a guy there that I had seen all summer but I wasn't pursuing because of Marc. Finally I decided to see what it was all about. I don't know what I did, but he responded. And I loved the attention. You could tell he was from Boston. And totally different. He was a doorman at a very swank place. It was really neat. He tried everything to get me. He serenaded me. He stood outside my window at this dormitory with sixty waitresses and he sang to me (laughs). I just couldn't handle it. Remember, I was still this virgin and I thought he just wanted to sleep with me. He tried everything. I wish he would come back! (laughs). What a waste!

Sex was so scary then. I didn't even know what a naked man looked like. I have no brothers. And my mother had made the guilt thing so bad. Women were pure and men were just after sex. I was thirteen years old before I found out what it was all about. I got my period one night washing the dishes and my mother said, "Okay, now I'm going to tell you how it gets done." There was no mention of love or feelings or how nice it could be or any of that. It was just this is what they do to you and you could get pregnant and don't you let anyone do that to you. I went ice-skating that night and I told all my girl friends. And nobody believed me. Somebody said, "But my father sleeps on the couch every night and my mother sleeps upstairs. When do they do it?" Incredible. And Marc grew up that same way. He never forced it.

Marc and I didn't see a whole lot of each other during those next few years, but we wrote and he was always somewhere in my mind. He was wandering from job to job and school to school. To a lot of people, Marc seemed lost, drifting around like that. But we were all doing nothing special either, just going to school. And he was really trying to find himself. He's very pure, if you know what I mean. And the beautiful thing was he always had himself. I loved him for that especially.

I graduated from school in 1961 and then our entire family moved from Maine to Boston on a Greyhound bus *(laughs)*. The "Real McCoys." I had stars in my eyes. I was going to get a job in the big city. And within two weeks, I had one working for the daily newspaper. I was nineteen years old, but even if I was supposedly successful, Marc was always in the back of my mind. You have to remember that the whole time I lived in Boston, I kept thinking that there had to be some way that I could get him.

Anyway, I had been in Boston for a year and had my own apartment when I got a wedding invitation from someone back home, and I went. Marc was there, and he was very impressed with me. I invited him over to my aunt's house and we spent the night together.

The physical attraction was still there. I remember sleeping on my aunt's couch and feeling very good. I got the prize again. He was the person I knew the most and loved and trusted. And I thought, If I act a certain way—really cool—I'll get him again. I've always felt that with Marc I have to hold myself back. Some part of me wants to just devour him. Just like when you have an infant, you want to bite its little fanny and its little arms. But I played it cool.

I went back to Boston and Marc went back to Rhode Island. And I got a letter from him, saying he wanted to visit me on Thanksgiving. I think I threw that letter up in the air and jumped up and down. Even my two roommates were excited. And then, the night before he was supposed to come, he called me up to tell me he's not coming. And I mean, I completely blew my three months' cool *(laughs)*. He said he didn't have any clean clothes. So I said, "Well look, why don't you just bring all your clothes and we'll go to the Laundromat and we'll wash them." I get very practical, and don't pay any attention to what he's really saying. I figure if I'm smart, he'll still come, but at this point I'm about ready to cry. And no, he's not coming. That's it. No clean clothes. So finally I said, "Okay. So don't come. Never mind. Just don't come." And then he said, "Well, I think I'll come." He was really putting me through it. What he's really saying is, "Are you willing to take me with all my problems, with what I'm really like?" And I said, "Yes!"

He came to Boston and we fell madly in love again. Boston was like magic land. We went around the city and took pictures of each other everywhere, doing all kinds of crazy things. We were really in love. He stayed at my house, which my mother didn't like. She didn't know if we're getting it on or not. With my hang-ups—I'm as safe as if I were in jail. It was still wonderful. I cooked him dinners. He came every weekend after that. We talked about a lot of things: "Life" and "What does it all mean?" and "We're so far from home."

And then one night, I was home with my two roommates and the phone rang and it was Marc. He was very drunk. And he was telling me how much he loved me. And then he said, "Look—I've decided that I think we should get married." It's funny, I'd waited for that for years and yet—this will sound very strange—I didn't feel anything. Then he came to Boston and we really talked and decided we would do it. We set a date for the following October and we planned that we would each give $1,000 to the marriage or some ridiculous plan. It ended up that we didn't have a cent *(laughs)*. The money that we got on our wedding day, which came up to maybe $100, was all the money that we had. And that's what we took to go on our honeymoon.

The rest of the year I worked in Boston and he'd gone to live at his uncle's in Bridgeport, Connecticut. He got a job painting tractors. I didn't really think about that too much. I mean, I just knew that someday he'd be a provider and a father and we'd have that home we always wanted.

The wedding was at Our Lady of the Good Counsel in Boston, a beautiful church. I was nervous and happy and excited. I was becoming Mrs. Marc Bricmont. He was the big one that I was catching. A prize. The wanderer. All the friends came from Maine and were really happy. They all loved me and loved Marc and for them it was the culmination of a high school romance. For them, we were like this perfect couple.

We had that $100 and off we went to Toronto. I was very young and very innocent. I was just being taken along. I had a flower on, and I think we stopped to eat at Howard Johnson's and I took it off. I really looked like a bride and it was embarrassing. I was proud, but I didn't want everybody to know. And there was the fact that we had to find a place to sleep and the whole thing. You know—it's really going to happen now. After all those years, it's going to really happen now. Somehow it's supposed to be magic that's going to happen to me now.

It was a horrible hotel. We heard people on the other side and I was so scared. We tried, but it didn't happen on the first night. I was, like, forget it, closed up. It went on like that for about three days. Finally we were in Montreal and we didn't know what to do, so we went to see an Elvis Presley movie in the middle of the afternoon. In the middle of it, Marc grabbed my arm and he said, "Come on—it's going to happen now. This is it. Enough bullshit." He got really angry. And off we went to wherever we were staying and it happened. But there certainly wasn't any pleasure. Forget pleasure *(laughs)*. There wasn't any joy. There wasn't any beauty. There wasn't any romance. But there was a feeling of accomplishment and I was so happy that it had happened that I was jumping up and down *(laughs)*. I wasn't even disappointed really because I never knew what to expect. I never even thought that it would be nice. It was just something that you did. Just having him close had always been enough.

I gave up my apartment. I said good-bye to my friends and my job and I went to his life in Plainville, Connecticut. Which was just that *(laughs)*. We lived upstairs in a little atticky place and an old couple lived downstairs. And sometimes I'd think, "What in God's name am I doing in this place with this man who goes off to paint tractors?" I was so lonely. But then he'd come home and I'd make him dinner. Sometimes he'd go off with his friends to play hockey and I would be just like a puppy. "Please take me." I'd go to the games and cheer. I just wanted to be wherever he was.

In those days, he would tell me his feelings about things. We would lie in bed in that funny little place and he'd talk. But it would have to be very dark so that I couldn't see his face and he didn't want to look in my eyes. We had a birthday party there for him too. One of his buddies, one of the guys he loved the most, came to stay with us, and I baked him a birthday cake and at midnight we took the cake out and sang "Happy Birthday." He was overwhelmed. Like it was the most love that he had gotten from anybody in his life. I was almost sorry that I'd done it because he couldn't handle being loved so much. But I needed to do it for someone. I remember before we got married he gave me a pewter beer mug with a glass bottom and he had engraved on it "To my bride." And that first Christmas I found the same mug somewhere at a store and I had "To my husband" engraved on it. It was beautiful.

By December, I wanted to have a baby. I mean, that's what our whole ultimate plan was, you know. To get married and have children. We visited my parents for Christmas and we made love there and I got pregnant. I was ecstatic. By that time we were living in a sweet little apartment in Bridgeport. We had friends. Marc was a housepainter. It was wonderful.

Pierre was born the following fall. I think it was the most wonderful day of my life. I loved my body. It was full and beautiful. On the day I gave birth I was incredibly calm, but Marc was a wreck. I had to keep telling him to relax. Everything was going to be all right. I was more worried about him than about me. Would you believe it? And then Pierre was born and it was a miracle. I wanted a boy so bad. I'd had all these sisters, you know. And Marc wanted a boy and we were just so happy. So, so happy.

I loved being a mother. I'm the mother type, I guess. I spent a lot of time with Pierre and so did Marc. But he was beginning to hate his job and one day he came home and he said, "All right. I quit the job." I had to admire him for it. I was scared, but he said he'd heard about this school in Florida that trained you to be an umpire. That's what he really wanted to do, so that's what we did. We packed up Pierre and all this baby stuff and put us all in a car and went to umpire school in Daytona Beach, Florida. Just like that.

We were there for a couple of months. And then Marc got a job in the minor leagues in the Midwest. His pay was going to be something like $250 a month and that didn't include expenses, which was a hotel room every night and three meals a day and travel. They had to go from one end of a four-hundred-mile radius to the other with baseball games. Seven days a week. But we were very excited about the job.

He went alone and said he'd send for me and finally he called me. He said, "You can't come here. It doesn't make any sense if I tell you what kind of life I'm living." I was really brokenhearted, but I understood. So I stayed for five months with my family in Boston, which was not easy to do. I got a job as a cocktail waitress near where my parents lived and I made a lot of money. And I was sending it to him to live on.

When Marc came back, I didn't even ask if he was faithful. The only answer would be no. And he knew it and it would have shattered me. So I didn't ask. Anyway, we were just so glad to be back together. He wasn't cut out for that sort of life, you know. No home. And he got a reputation for being a tough umpire. He would send me clippings—"the fastest thumb in the Midwest" (laughs).

We found an apartment for ourselves in Boston. It was like a dungeon. We were having a hard time every which way. We hadn't been together for five months. This baby was there and he was getting bigger. He was a year old or so. And what was Marc going to do with himself? Does he go off and be a baseball umpire the next season or do we forget about that for a while? He was trying all kinds of weird jobs. He sold encyclopedias for a while and they didn't give him the money they promised. All this kind of thing.

And yet I remember good times with friends. People coming over for dinner. My whole thing was the family. I just wanted us to be together. Like I'd say, Can we all go for a walk or something together. I'd always be trying to drag Marc off to Boston Common or down by the Charles. And as soon as we would all be walking off together, I was instantly happy. That's all it took. Marc always made me feel like I was dragging him around. But then he'd let go and we'd start laughing and play ball and that was fine. To see him and Pierre play ball together—it just would make my heart feel good.

We built furniture together. I would get great ideas. We made everything ourselves. We painted trees on the wall. I had a great idea for a headboard to be made out of wrought iron. Marc went around everywhere looking for one but he couldn't find any. So I said, All right, we're going to go to a junkyard and we'll get pipes and you can weld them together. And he made this beautiful thing. And we had colorful cube tables. When you walked into our house there was this real nice feeling there.

And then I got pregnant again. That really did it for me with the church, to put it mildly. We had one kid already and we could hardly manage. Not just money. I don't care so much about money. But four people instead of three. Not knowing what we were doing. When I got pregnant, I wanted to absolutely kill myself. Marc was miserable too. We felt completely powerless. But after a few months I just accepted the fact that I was pregnant and I went to work as a waitress because we were just about starving. I was pregnant and waiting on tables and standing on my feet and taking care of Pierre besides. It was insanity. I was just like a machine.

We started to fight a lot. We hurt each other. And we did it really good. The way that I used to be able to get at him was that I could talk more easily than he could. I'm more verbal. And when we would start arguing, he had no chance. I would come up with so many good words so fast that I left his head spinning and he would just completely go off into the twilight zone and not talk to me. That made it five hundred times worse than if he had been fighting back. I would be so beaten down by his silence.

Leslie was born in 1967 and that was a beautiful birth too. I didn't want a girl, but the first time they brought her to me and put her in my arms, it was instant communication and instant love. But the friction between Marc and me was just getting so enormous. These two little kids both in diapers. I don't have a washing machine and I don't drive a car. I have to go grocery shopping with two infants. I can't believe that they're ever going to get older. I've turned into a workhorse. Marc at this point is working all day for an airline and comes home into this scene. Sometimes he doesn't come home. We also don't have enough money, so I got a job at Kay's Ice Cream Parlor five nights a week. I'd get home at two every night and take care of the kids the next day. I just kept going and tried not to think. You know—do what you have to do. And yet if somebody had said to me, Okay, you can give up Marc and give up the kids and be totally free, I wouldn't have done it. I wouldn't have known what to do or where to go. I loved them. Even now, when my children are staying with their father and I'm all alone and I can play records, it has no meaning. It's just for me and that isn't enough. It's too empty, you know.

Marc was doing the best he could. No, I never wanted to marry someone else. Someone else is going to have their own problems. Maybe there would be more money, maybe they'd know how to handle things better, but then they'd have something else wrong with them. And the love was there, the feeling was there and that was enough.

I remember when we took walks I would hold his arm. We were always this very beautiful-looking couple. People liked looking at us. We would meet somebody and it would turn out that they'd been looking at us for a year and dying to meet us. We started to have a lot of friends then who were Boston intellectuals. They were all in therapy and they loved hearing stories about Auburn.

We were still these small-town kids together and we would always be that way. I remember walking down the street together when there was no money and maybe I was pregnant or whatever. I remember Marc saying, "How are they all doing it, all the rest of them out there? How come we're having such a hard time? What's the matter with us? Are we so different? Why can't we make it?"

It wasn't the money that was bothering him. It was something else, but I could never figure out what. I could have taken anything except for the loneliness. Silence. Talk to me. Tell me what you're feeling. Help! When we would have fights, it would be me saying, "Will you say something?" And I'd hit him. I mean, we were really starting to have fights and I would break windows. I was going to kill myself. I remember a couple of fights in front of the kids—I was really vicious—I'd hit him as hard as I could. But it was just to get a reaction.

One night I called him on the phone from work. I said, "You don't care if I come home, do you?" I was asking for it. And he says, "No, I don't." I slammed the phone down and I said to myself, "There's no way that I'm going to go home to that man." I didn't know where to go, so I just went home with the busboy. He was a real pig, but it was better than nothing. At least somebody had their arms around me. I came home at seven in the morning. Marc sort of looks over and goes back to sleep. No words, no nothing.

Then Marc got promoted at the airline. He became a sales representative. And all of a sudden he was making $12,000 a year. And had an expense account. But we still didn't spend that much time together. Through the airline he was taking a lot of trips. He went to Portugal for a week by himself. He went to Russia and he didn't want me to come. The trust was going. I didn't really allow myself to think that there were other women. I just couldn't. He was getting very sophisticated too, very cool. Business lunches and friends I didn't know and phone calls. And I was keeping the little home going and working hard and being the dutiful wife.

Finally, we went on a cruise together in the Caribbean. My girl friend Sally took care of the children. But we had a miserable time. We were uptight. We tried to fit into this groove and it's not really us. And sex was bad. If you don't take care of your relationship, then when you finally do get time together, you just don't know what to do with it.

Sometimes sex had been good and sometimes it wasn't. After Pierre was born was the best. But I didn't have enough orgasms. And that always made me feel bad. He would say I was frigid. I believed it too. And the only kind of lovemaking that I wanted to do was plain ordinary stuff. I didn't want to try anything else because it wasn't comfortable and it just wasn't me. Marc wasn't comfortable either. It was just like that was what we were supposed to get into. We would talk and I told him what I liked. There were definite positions and things that I liked better. Marc knew what they were, but I think that he was very bored with it all. And I felt frustrated a whole lot.

Then Marc quit his job at the airlines. He was just fed up, you know, so he took a job as a cabdriver. I got a job waiting on tables at a place in town. Summer was coming, and God, we had been in Boston for five years or so. I was nervous about spending another summer there. Taking the kids to these rotten pools. Getting around on the subways. Getting them cooled off in the sprinkler and then by the time you got home they were hot again. I was really trapped. Marc wasn't coming home nights from the cab job. And self-preservation just sort of took over. I decided I would get a job out on the North Shore. Hire myself out as a governess. I know how to take care of children and I know how to take care of a home. I would definitely be an asset to have around. But I had to have my children with me. I wanted fresh air and a beach for them. And I worked out this whole thing in my head and when I felt that I had something, I presented it to Marc.

"I'm going," I said, "and I'm taking the kids to the shore and you can have this apartment and do whatever you want to do. Whatever you've always wanted to do." And you know, I scared the hell out of him.

"It's all going to change," he said. "What about if we *all* go somewhere? I really want us to stay together. Let's just go far away. Let's go to the North Shore, the whole family."

I said, "Gee—I've never been there. Do you think we could do it?"

And he said, "Yes."

But it was over, really. We went up to the North Shore and we tried and I still had some hope, but he didn't really want to be with me.

Finally we set a date for him to leave. It was breaking my heart. He was so anxious to go. And meanwhile—this was now the beginning of spring—I met another guy at the beach. Ed was crazy about me. He was so nice and loving. He was going to move in when Marc left. But he wasn't Marc.

Then the week before Marc's supposed to pack and leave, we're in the garden raking leaves and I fell in some real funny way and broke my arm. I was screaming with pain and he ran over and—you won't believe this—he yelled at me. "How could you be so stupid!" All he could think of was whether it was going to mess up his leaving. I had to go to the hospital and everything. He practically never came to visit me. It was just one more emergency that he couldn't handle.

When I came out of the hospital, he picked me up and took me home. And he left the same day. It was a beautiful sunny day and I tried to stay away from him while he finished packing. I couldn't stop crying, but I didn't want him to see. Ed was coming over after and some friends and I just kept trying to think of that.

He left on his bicycle. I stood on the porch and I watched him go. It was like a movie, you know. The tears were streaming down my face and he rode away and then he got smaller and smaller and then I couldn't see him anymore. And you know what I felt, really? When he disappeared? I felt relief. I miss him now. But then I just felt this enormous relief.

The other day I was with my friend Ariel and we went past Marc's house and he was in the yard. And we talked a little bit and then Ariel and I left and she said, "Who is that guy—he really loves you." When I told her, she couldn't believe it.

I gave him everything I had. Maybe I should have held back more. I don't know. It's so strange. I mean, here I am, I'm at the peak of my life and my sexuality, right? I want somebody to sleep with, to love me. I told him awhile ago that I'd love him forever, you know. I'm yours, if you ever want me. I've stopped now. It's not good for me. He comes here and he's uncomfortable and I'm not doing one thing to make him comfortable. He's on his own. I'm not making any moves in his direction, or any man's direction for that matter. I'm not taking any chances. It's too precarious. Right now I'm just trying to get my own life together in this new place. It's pretty lonely, but it's mine. It's warm and there's food, the kids. There's friends. It's beginning to look like a home.

Marc Bricmont makes a strong physical impression. He spends much of his time working out-of-doors, and his athletic body and handsome face create a robust image. He is an erratic talker, given to long, dreamy silences followed by sudden rushes of words. Born in Auburn thirty-two years ago, he was raised in the same neighborhood as Michele from eleven onward. He now lives with a girl friend in an unheated room in the same small town as Michele and their children.

MARC:
We met in high school, around sixteen, I guess. She was more, I'd say, emotionally mature. And she was exterior with her feelings. So when we met, she voiced some attraction to me. My immediate impulse was shyness. I pulled back for a month or so. And then, so far as I remember what

happened, we had a football game—it was out of town—and we happened to be on the same bus. We more or less got to know each other, and she voiced her attraction to me again. So we started dating, steady dating so we didn't date anyone else. We went out on Friday and Saturday nights. Also, on weeknights I'd usually go to her home and we'd sit around and watch TV and once her parents went up to bed we'd pet. We'd do everything but really make love.

I guess you'd say it was more or less love immediately. Passion and the whole thing. I was possessed by it. Before, when I went out with girls, it was just to romance. But this was the first emotional kind of thing—the first time I ever touched somebody's insides, you know. We would discuss our feelings.

I was a loner. I would always solve my own problems instead of going to someone. I had this inner world. Except for the ball field and the rink. That was a different story, I was always much looser there. I could totally experience myself in any game. And I never really found that total ease anywhere else besides with Michele. I mean, in the presence of others, I just can't let go. Even with the girl I am with now, I hide parts of myself—some fear or doubt—but with Michele the beautiful thing was I never felt like I had to change. I got that same kind of freedom with Michele that I got on the rink.

Still, there was a lot of conflict between being with your girl and being with the guys. It was a thing of if you expressed your feelings with a girl, they'd call you on it. Not a sissy, but some word like that. Like at a high school dance, you were always more or less reserved in front of the guys. You would be on your guard of letting the girl direct or tell you what to do. You know, very cool.

One thing I remember very well from those days was all that petting. It went on for hours after her parents went to bed. We'd go through the whole thing and then I'd feel I wanted to go and there was usually a scene. I'd have to go to bed, but most times she wasn't ready for me to go. She wasn't satisfied, she wanted more and I'd just had it. She'd go into tears, You can't go! and that would make me close up more and I'd just want to get out of there. She'd hang on me and lock the door. She wouldn't let me go. I think the first time we broke up was that kind of scene.

But we'd meet between classes after we broke up. She still had an attraction for me and me for her. We'd say hello. Sometimes I'd see her and go the other way. But she'd always just be there and say, "Let's go to lunch," or "Why don't you come over tonight?" I didn't have to take any actions, because she did everything. It made me feel secure, you know, to think, That person still loves me. It's a nice feeling.

I remember one time we broke up and we got back together again at a basketball game in Boston. I'd gone up by bus and she'd come up with friends. Somehow we met in the streets of Boston and we went to a small café and had lunch and we talked about our feelings. It was so warm. It felt good to feel that again. I guess, even when we didn't see each other that feeling in my guts was always there.

We were both virgins at the time. It didn't really matter to me. I didn't want to force anything. I always guessed what I was doing was what everyone else was doing. I remember then Michele had firm, you know, breasts. She was considered big-breasted compared to the other girls and that was commented on. One time I was sitting in front of a friend in English class and he sort of nudged me in the back and said, "Hey! Are you still playing with Michele's big tits?" I just turned around and swung as hard as I could. He apologized afterward. I felt good about that.

We had this thing where we'd say Michele was strength and I was pride, and together we could do most anything. There was total freedom whether it was just horseplay or making out. There were never any inhibitions. No ego things, where you present a different image for your ego.

We accepted each other as is. I think that tightness will never change, that union of feeling just continues. I'd had that fantasy since I was a little kid, to find a woman and to find that kind of closeness. My thoughts then were sort of religious about it. I'd think, "God, if You'll only grant me a woman I can marry and have children with." I wanted that family, that unit or whatever.

Her family was very warm. I felt more comfortable in her home than in mine, so I'd spend most of my time at her place. Every Sunday, I'd have dinner there, plus any time I happened to be there I'd eat with them. And during that time when her father was away, I'd eat there a lot. Sort of the man in the house. I didn't feel awkward with them, even with her little sisters. It was very harmonious. I could always express more to Michele's mother than to my own mother.

On Sundays, we'd meet on the corner there in the mornings—halfway up the block—and we'd go to church together, just the two of us. I hadn't really thought much about church before that.

I guess I am not a person who plans things very well and so things seem to happen by surprise. After high school, all my friends went to college and I was the one who stayed in Auburn. They all had athletic scholarships and I could have had one too, but I was penniless, so it wouldn't have been enough. There was no possible way. It made me feel very alone, very bitter. And then Michele said she was going down to junior college and that was like the end. I remember driving her down there. It was like going to war or something, leaving her there, thinking about how we were going to miss each other and how life would not be the same. I felt empty. She cried and I cried.

I got a job working in the maintenance department of a mental institution. My outlet then was I played ice hockey on this local team and we played teams from all over New England and Canada. You weren't supposed to get paid because it was amateur hockey, but at the end of the year you were paid, you know, what they called expense money. It felt good to be on that team, but I missed her. I missed someone being concerned, loving me. My pals were gone. There were a couple of girl friends I'd meet at this local bar, but nobody to love. Just a good time. But I don't recall it as any lonelier than most other times.

Those three or four years after high school were all like that, just wasting time. No direction or anything or motivation. I didn't see Michele much. I scraped some money together and went to school for a while in the South and then to a little college in Providence. I thought I was having a pretty good time in school there. You know, living with three or four guys and everything was fine. Well, it was during this time that I went up to Auburn for a wedding and there was Michele and she said, "Look, come down to Boston for Thanksgiving and I'll make you a dinner." I told her that the chances are I wouldn't make it and then at the last moment I changed my mind and really wanted to do it. All the other fellows were going home or to their girls, so I just said, Why not?.I was never close enough to my family to go back for Thanksgiving.

It is true that that weekend changed my life. I took the bus down and she met me. She had been in Boston six or seven months on her own and had a Boston life going and knew all the local pubs. She showed me her womanness and the class she had. We went to her apartment and she cooked this beautiful Italian dinner, just for the two of us, and then we lay back in bed and made love—but didn't make love—and we slept in the same bed and it was the feeling of just waking up in the middle of the night and having someone warm next to you and just curling over and hugging. It was a wonderful feeling. I kept thinking, This is what it's all about! Like there is no loneliness here. It's so alive and warm.

Also, you see, it was her grounds. She knew it and impressed me with it. She was independent and had a job on a newspaper and an apartment. So she again reminded me of strength. And I thought, I could grow with her, you know. I don't want to tag along with her, but she's someone I felt proud of. That weekend just warmed me up completely. She was like a complete home, I guess you could say.

After this great weekend, just getting on a bus and going back to Providence and feeling lost and low, I asked myself, "What am I going back to Providence for?" And when I got back I said, "What am I doing here? This will end in nothing. Michele, she's the one for me." I got very carried away with it. When I got home I called her up and said, "Let's get married." And her immediate reaction was, "What? Are you crazy? What's happened to you?" And I like just insisted on it. She was really surprised. I mean, we hadn't really seen much of each other for all that time and after that one weekend I wanted to get married. She was having a good life there, dating rugby players and thinking of going to Australia. I said, "We're getting married and that's it. I don't want to hear anything else."

I really needed her, I needed those things we shared. I saw marriage as a fulfilling thing. Getting married was a thing I always wanted to do. And it was a marriage made in heaven. It was a union of feelings. There was a brother-sisterhood about it. I say that because it was equal. I was not above or below her.

In January, before we got married, I moved to Bridgeport and lived with my uncle and worked for him as an operating engineer on a Caterpillar. And then we got married in Boston. I remember it was a good day, all but one of my old friends were there. And then we spent five or six days on the honeymoon and went to Bridgeport to live. We lived in a small upstairs apartment and in the beginning Michele didn't work and I'd go off to work and she'd do dinners. It was very warm, very comfortable.

We had a special thing going together in Bridgeport because we came from another place together. We had this like common bond that everybody else just wondered about. Our expressions and the way we acted. I think we put on less airs than other people did. We spoke in more what I call an honest way.

Once we were married, our sex life was happy. Just beginning to really know sex and how to express it and lose some of our guilt and fears and all. We sort of discovered sex together. I got such comfort and joy from it. And it was more spontaneous than with any other girl. I had less shyness with her.

We didn't use any birth control or anything of that nature. Once we started lovemaking it was just, Whatever happens, happens. So when she got pregnant with Pierre, it was by accident, but not really. I totally accepted it and was very, very happy about it. I remember the doctor called me at home to tell me Pierre was born and I felt such joy I cried real tears. We were doing OK.

There was something, though: I don't think I was very happy with my job, but I really enjoyed playing ice hockey one or two days a week with this team in Bridgeport. And if we had a game at night, my mind was already on the game in the afternoon. The only thing which would concern me was getting prepared, you know, mentally, for the game. So I'd come home after work and maybe not be so expressive or want to get into some kind of communication. And then a stir would be created. "What's the matter with you?" she'd say. I remember one night—it was before a championship game and all my thoughts and energies were getting ready for that—she demanded some talk from me. She got me into such an emotional state I finally left her at home. We lost the game by one goal. And I blame her. I was practically useless on the ice. After that game, I didn't want to come home.

Around that time I got involved in baseball umpiring. I took another job, housepainting, so I could do it. First I umpired high school- and college-level games. Then I hoped to do it professionally, so we went down to Al Samera's Umpire School in Daytona Beach. I did well in that school. There were sixty students and I was third in the class, so I got my choice of jobs in the minor league. I liked that work even better than playing ball. The authority and decision-making. It was a battle at first getting their respect because usually an umpire is older than the players.

Things were really looking up for us then. The plan was I was going to work the Midwest circuit, go out there and make some sort of a·home. Then, that didn't make any sense because I wouldn't have seen her more than one or two days a month and I wasn't making enough money, so she stayed in Boston and worked. I missed her and Pierre so much during that time. It was cold, staying in hotels. But I was really deep into my work. I met women on the road, but I was always faithful. Finally I decided my family is what I wanted and just came home for good at the end of the season.

That's when we all started living together in Boston in a little basement. It was a long way from Auburn. I didn't know what to do then. I'd play ball in the park or just wander around the streets. Living day to day. Michele didn't complain or bug me about that. She was a good wife that way. She never asked me to get it together. We never worried about money. Things always got paid somehow. It just happened. That period between Pierre and Leslie was just good between us. So far as sex was concerned, it was our best period. She had had a child and was freer. We were compatible and whole together.

Michele was more upset than I when Leslie was born. For me, it felt warm, but she never gave Leslie the same feeling of love she gave Pierre. I probably mothered Leslie more than Michele did because of that.

Then I got this peon job with TWA making telephone calls. I looked around and saw other people working at other levels and I asked the guy, "How do you get that job?" And he said, "It takes three years." I said, "I can do it now." And I got it. I was a salesman. I tripled my salary and got an American Express Card expense account. I went to conventions and meetings. It was a big change from odd jobs and baby-sitting. But it didn't really change our life much. It was just another thing. I only worked a couple hours a day, bullshit, came home and jumped in bed with Michele, then came back to the office. It was the easiest job I ever had.

Sometimes I just couldn't be a husband or a father. I couldn't go to the park on Sunday and be a happy family. It's funny. I wanted a family. I'm so glad I have kids. I just don't know what to do with them. But when I did wander off for a day in the streets, my thoughts were always at home. Then I'd come home and Michele would say, "Welcome home," and I would feel the pleasure of that because I really loved her, you know, but after a few hours it's all satisfied and I'd want to be alone again.

Sometimes I try to explain to myself why I should have this struggle. Like there is a doughnut shop in town here now where I used to go every morning before work and have some coffee. I'd talk to this couple who run the shop about what I was doing. And then one day I didn't go in. And the next day the man said, "Hey, where were you yesterday?" and I didn't go back in there ever again.

We did have some very good times too, family times. We liked to drive off to the beach with the kids on Sundays, just sea and sun, then come home, put the kids to bed early and eat and make love and read newspapers. You know, just feel comfortable. And Michele used to say, "See, you're not a wanderer. You have a family here." I'd feel guilty that I couldn't always be this man that she wanted, this father, this family man. She always wanted more. Like more feelings. She was saying, Feel! Express! Love! Show love! And the more she would get into this, the more I would want to be free. To run away and be in the streets. I really could not understand what it was I wasn't giving. One time it came to me that what I wasn't giving just wasn't part of me. She was crying for something I didn't have to give her. I think that burned something out in me and it made me more restless as those times went on.

I guess it was around then that Michele started complaining that I am not satisfying her in bed. I couldn't understand. I wasn't doing anything different. I had the same feelings. I don't make love just to make love. I carried on as normally as I could, not ever understanding what was wrong. For a while there, everything was fine and Michele was having those so-called orgasms, but now she said it was bad. There was a certain time of day in the afternoon when she was ready for lovemaking, and at that moment in what do you call it, passion, there was no problem. That's why I figured, when it didn't work, it was a problem in her cycle or whatever.

Sometimes, traveling on my own, I would wonder if I would be attractive to other women. And so I would be with them. In Portugal and in the Caribbean. I did very little screwing around. It just happened. I hated deceiving Michele. I felt soiled by it. If I could have just said, "Look, I screwed someone, that's all I did and it didn't mean anything," then it would have been OK. But I couldn't say such a thing. I was afraid she would totally blow up and it would be an end-of-the-world kind of thing. So instead I gave her half the truth, but she never really picked it up.

Then, I quit that airline job and all that phoniness and drove a cab and I started to really feel good. I had that total freedom of going where I wanted, eating where I wanted, seeing a movie if I wanted. I didn't have any affairs. I was content just with that freedom and working at night. We didn't see much of each other, just bumped into each other in the mornings and nights. And I was starting to get a sort of strength on my own, something for myself. And then Michele was not able to make me feel guilty so much anymore. And it was around then I started speaking of separation.

I guess from then on I was just biding my time. I couldn't just break away. I always thought of her as a good person, an attractive person, a person with a lot of strength and words. But then I would look at her and say, She's not a good-looking person. Or I would just see this babbling woman. I would create these ideas. They were just ways to give me reasons to leave.

Our plan was to move up to the North Shore and wait for the spring to separate. I felt guilt-ridden about it, especially if Michele cried or showed me her love. I would say to Michele, "If I'm not fulfilling you, why do you want me?" I didn't really love her now, except on the spur of the moment.

Finally we were going to split up. There was all that anxiety because we were actually going to leave each other after talking about it for so long. And then, one afternoon, Michele and I were raking the yard and all of a sudden she's yelling my name and I turn around and she's down on the ground screaming. It was a week before we were going to separate and I kept thinking, You aren't supposed to get hurt at a time like this. Get hold of yourself. I called the rescue squad and she needed surgery.

But now this is strange. You see, what I didn't know was Michele started seeing this lover, Ed, and although I took her to the hospital and the whole thing, it was switched around. I'd be at her bedside, trying to show compassion or whatever, and she'd be removed because her mind was on him. He was the one who took her through recuperation. She didn't need me anymore. And I was angry, because all of a sudden, I'm not number one anymore. Even in that tragic period when I should be at her side, he had taken over my job completely. I started getting panicky about it and having doubts about what I was doing. I started questioning myself, but I knew what I was doing was right, that I was just going through the death of it.

Some nights, after that, I would get so unbelievably lonely that I would just have to talk to her. I'd plead with her to talk with me. I was so totally pained and I'd want a reconciliation, but I wouldn't really. One of those times I even convinced Michele to go to bed with me, but we didn't make love because she was so removed. And she said, "This is the last time. I can't do this anymore."

It's strange, isn't it? I had been so afraid for so long to make this move and now she immediately had all these friends and this lover and I was totally alone. It changed me. It opened me in some ways.

I have no regrets. Of all the women I have known, I could not have shared those years or what happened with anyone who could have given me any more or fulfilled me more. I know we'll never get together again into a relationship. I would say if I were to just let go and, say, hold her or get my feelings out—if I didn't block that out—I could still get that same feeling back as before. But I do want to block it out. Because besides that feeling there is also relating to her. I mean, besides this union with someone, you also have to live with them and that can be hard.

JOHN AND PATTI
Chronology

1965	John and Patti meet at a psychology seminar in Pittsburgh.
1966	They live together in San Francisco.
1967	They marry.
1969	Rebecca is born.
1971	Their open marriage begins.
1972	The engagement party to announce their group marriage to another couple.
1973	They separate.

8

Open
Marriage

The myth of Open Marriage takes an appraising look at the role of matrimony in a liberated society and comes up with a radically new concept. Open Marriage is marriage without compromise or self-denial. It is the joint experiment of two people who grow and change by planning and participating in each other's independence. The only rules in this marriage are the ones the husband and wife make together. Together, they break new ground and live the ultimate marital adventure.

After five years of marriage, John Spinelli and Patricia Manning decided that they could have a more fulfilling relationship and more exciting individual lives by embarking on an Open Marriage.

At fifty-one, Dr. John Spinelli has a national reputation as a psychiatrist, author, lecturer, and liberal political activist. He is a short, strongly built man with a full head of curly white hair, a white beard, and an incredibly youthful face. He speaks rapidly, jumping from one subject to another effortlessly. Dr. Spinelli lives with a woman in his own house in San Francisco and shares the care of his daughter, Rebecca, with his former wife.

JOHN:

I marry a lot. I've never wanted to live alone. Folks used to say to me, "John, you really should try it on your own. You're just escaping your fear of living alone." But then I suddenly realized, Sure, I can live alone. I could also cut my leg off. I just don't like it.

I've lived with a woman for as long as I can remember. I was married at nineteen. My first marriage was a lovely, friendly, delicious growing-up period. That lasted seven years. And my second marriage was about fifteen years. With her I had four children, built a career, ambition, the whole thing. She was unhappy about the way it came out; that was before the real consciousness developed and she got into being herself a little too late. So you understand I am for marriage—early and often. I'm not romantic about marriage, but I wouldn't marry unless someone turns me on. I figure there are 200 million people in this country and I could make it with 10 to 15 million of them. But if you focus on one relationship, you grow and learn from it.

I was separated from my second wife at the time I met Patti. She was a student in a seminar I gave as a visiting lecturer in Pittsburgh. I thought she had the biggest, most beautiful tits in the world. When I saw her walking down that room, I said to myself, "If I don't get a nibble of that tit before I die, my life will be less." She was all the different experiences I had never had. A total WASP. And she was most responsive. In fact, she pursued me. I was the professor, daddy, superstar, and she was being a groupie, I guess. She was married at the time and I became the route to do what she wanted to do. She was very focused, determined, tenacious. And quite soon she decided I was it. I certainly cannot be described as a fish hooked against my will; I was a fish hooked for my will.

She was a bright young woman, very pretty, a good body,

and she fucked lovely. She knew where she wanted to go so I did the big mentor trip. In many ways she was like a doll to me. I treated her, took her out, bought clothes for her, and dressed her because she dressed like Minneapolis Junior League. I got her into the whole San Francisco scene. This is what the big city is all about. I remember the first time we went to a party in San Francisco I bought every stitch on her back for her. I didn't know if our relationship would last. She was heavy into dancing and not much into the kind of intellectual pursuits I was into. But in no time at all I was dancing and she was very heavy into content. She had a good head on her own.

I remember when I married her a few of my friends had raised eyebrows. You know, the twenty-year difference, and I'm an old-fashioned radical and she's a Goldwaterite. But I'd say, "Look, it'll last five years. So it's five years with a wonderful person. Who would turn down five years of now?" The natural half-life of marriage in our society is five years. Then you can renew to find your new significance—who you are then—or you get divorced. Many people think it's catastrophic—Patti's and my separation and divorce—but some remember that I said it was just good for five years. In choosing to be with Patti I had an overall sense that anything could happen, but whatever happened there would be a heightened consciousness.

Well, shit, the first month after I married Patti she ran off with another guy. She fell head over heels in love with her boss. She's heavy into parental males (laughs). I knew the day she slept with him. I was out in Sausalito with my kids, and with my own deliberate kind of Machiavellian manipulation, I called her when I knew she was in bed with the guy. She totally denied it. I said, "Look, I know what's going on. Now don't fuck your head over. There's no such thing as sin." It's not a moral thing, it just bothered me about the lying because I just can't stand to feel crazy. You know, either you're crazy or she's lying. I tried very hard to keep the relationship going. The fucking him was not so much a shitty thing. I could have worked through that part. I felt she had a lot of fucking around to do. You see, what really destroyed me is that she didn't know what she wanted. I only became outraged when she would not make up her mind and wouldn't talk to me about it. She wouldn't talk, she wouldn't screw.

Finally she came to me and she said she hadn't realized what love was, that she was crazy, but that she did love me. I felt that she was making a choice and I was very happy that she had gotten together where she was. Patti is very straight when she's talking. She said she was finished with this guy. She was committed to a one-to-one relationship without lying. We both really wanted to try a committed, ongoing relationship. Our conditions were that we would be open, direct, and honest with each other. She could do what she liked as long as we talked. Almost like an open church.

It has always been my feeling that there is no adult male-female relationship that can really expand into both people unless they have the experience of generativity. Because I don't think two people would ever stay together if they just had themselves. Then you get very narcissistic. You have to focus outside of yourself to stay together because at any moment there's somebody who screws better, who has a better hairstyle, a better complexion, doesn't fart as much, and is more admired. So what keeps you in the relationship is something beyond the moment. And besides that, I'm really nuts about babies. So we had Rebecca on plan. By decision.

From the day Becky came home from the hospital, I've taken half-time care of her, three and a half days every week. I think we both honestly tried to change around the parent-child thing, to acknowledge that each of us had an equal place in the relationship. That meant formal things like who cooked and who did the dishes. It really was something that I had been into since I was a kid because my "Old Lady" drove me crazy, my father crazy, my brother crazy, by not fulfilling herself. I've always felt that if a woman fulfills herself it's a better scene and she's not trying to tear it out of you. It took about a year of readjustments with hassles, but eventually I gave up my job teaching at the hospital and went back into private practice, so that I could work two days a week, and those were the days I wasn't on duty at home. We have lived that way ever since.

Patti really completed an education for me I could never have completed alone. I think that was a talent of hers. I learned. I grew. I enjoyed it. I feel that I got over the stereotype male stuff. Patti was good at sticking to that petty sort of division. It's almost as though if there were four dishes, I should wash two. And that wasn't bad. That was good. It was an irritant, it was very difficult to get accommodated to what I considered the higher order, but it got me in touch with how much I am into kids, how much I am into house and home, how much I am a mother.

Our sexual relationship was always there, always good. When we first married, we screwed every night. I'm a very ardent, active lover. I really dig sex a lot. There was one period when Patti was involved with this guy right after we were married where I began to have symptoms of premature ejaculation. And Patti absolutely cured me. The second time I had premature ejaculation, Patti just turned on me like an animal. She was hostile and nasty and said, "The next time you do that, I'm leaving." I blinked. I would have sworn premature ejaculation was an unconscious act, but Patti made it conscious and I never did it again after that. A total cure.

When our sex life began, Patti was very much into compliant performance; she wasn't concerned about feeling, herself. Right at the very beginning I confronted her about orgasm. She could do whatever she liked. She was only having orgasms about one out of three times and she had concerns about being a nymphomaniac because she wasn't satisfied. I told her her orgasms were hers and she could do whatever she liked about them. It was a big relief for Patti! I guess the first few years of our marriage was her getting out of that bag.

Then Patti wanted a house. She wanted stability. We had a long scene about that because I know what a house takes. I told Patti it would take a year and it would be very hard. When we bought the house, I worked on it every night until midnight or one o'clock. I was pretty exhausted and for that year I was less into sex. That was the year Patti got involved with her new boss. Patti maintained that she got involved with her boss because we didn't screw a lot. I maintain she got involved with her boss—*and* we didn't screw a lot.

It was a terribly tense time. I knew about it and confronted her a few times and she'd say, "No, I'm not in love with him." But she was. It drove me nuts. She would just lie out of her ears. She had learned to lie so good there was nothing I could do about it. She would call up and say, "I have to go to a meeting," or "I'm going to an office party on New Year's Eve." That was the New Year's just before we bought the house. She said, "I'm going to an office party. Can you come?" I said, "What the fuck are you doing, calling me at seven o'clock at night? What am I going to do with Rebecca? Dump her out the window? She's a baby, I can't drop her." "Well, I really have to go and I really want you to come if you want to and if you can find a sitter." Forget it. I was pissed with that. She didn't come back from that New Year's party until four in the morning. "Where were you?" "I was at the party." "Patti, you weren't at the party. I called at midnight to wish you a Happy New Year and you were gone." "Oh, we got onto the wrong bus and we had a flat." "Yeah!" "That's really what happened."

Now what's going on underneath is that she's saying to

herself, "I don't want to hurt him. Why should I hurt him? It's my own life. What's he doing in my own life? He's trying to control me." That it's a lie is insignificant to her. She's very self-righteous, because she's dealing with a higher principle: comfort. That's what I've always known about Patti—she's absolutely without any stable ethic. She'd do incredible scenes. I had a vasectomy shortly after Rebecca was born. Patti still had a diaphragm. Why does she have a diaphragm? We had a long discussion in which Patti points out that she feels trapped without one. She doesn't want to fuck around but she wants the right to. And you know, I'm believing her excuses because I can't deal with it any other way.

I'm certainly not opposed to fun fucking, but I'm not able to relate to another woman in terms of, "I really love you. Let's fuck . . . tell me you love me, I'm coming." I just can't do that. When I was married to my second wife, I did fuck around a lot. Very unpleasant. She was heavy into not fucking, withholding. So I really fucked around a lot in those years, which really saved my life in the sense that I found out what I had to find out—that it was her, not me. I swear, I got bursitis of the arms, diddling her until she would come.

Back to Patti. While she's fucking around, I tried fucking around once or twice myself. But I had too many things to do. I wanted to be with Becky. I wanted to take care of the house. I had my practice to do. Who's got time? I mean, I could fuck around easily if I could say, "Look, I have fifteen minutes between patients. Why don't we go have a friendly fuck?" That kind of thing is fine for me, but to think about the chasing—I really couldn't do it.

We were at the five-year half-life of the relationship. For me the decline part was the dishonesty. Just knowing that we couldn't be straight with each other in the area of sex was very frightening to us. We were just not dealing with what was. That was also the period that Patti was heavy into conducting sexuality workshops. I think she was getting in touch with the extent of her sexuality and how it was really very repressed. Now rather than feeling herself as a nymphomaniac, she was feeling herself as a full sexual person. Then one night we had a big party. Patti was talking about sexuality and she made a mistake. She said she realized that she had always considered herself a virgin even though she fucked around a lot. And only now had she really begun to feel free.

I felt tremendously elated that she let herself go in saying that. I saw it as an openness. Her up-front part was really such a turn-on. So I had a few drinks that night and we went upstairs and I told her how much I loved her and admired her for being that straight. That I absolutely adore her upfrontness.

"Listen," I said, "we have to find a way of getting things straightened out, because I really dig you when you are upfront. I'm going to tell you who I'm screwing and I know you fucked with this one and this one too." She acknowledged those things and then she talked about her sexual needs and how to deal with them. She wanted an open relationship and that's the way she could do it. It was clear that fundamentally she loved me and she had a plan for dealing with her needs for other men—group sex.

The group-sex thing was kind of a shock to me for a moment. I always considered it a kind of dirty Protestant scene, not something nice Catholic boys do. But when we talked about it, it seemed logical. I wouldn't have to be suspicious. I really got turned on to the whole thing. It was to be perfectly delightful. We read all the group-sex stuff. And talked to people. It was really kind of a joint conclusion. Our agreement was we would not screw with any other person individually, that we would only approach other couples.

It's a little embarrassing to talk about it now, but that experience worked fine for me. In fact, it probably was the central experience of my life. One of the main things I got out of it was that I got over sexual jealousy. Totally. I mean, I really wasn't jealous if she was screwing with someone I knew who was sort of a friend. And I found out that the best way to get out of your wife's crotch is to be in some other crotch. It keeps you occupied, you know. But the first big thing that happened to us is that our own sexual relationship exploded. Just contemplating all this alternate sexuality turned us both so hot that we must have screwed twenty-four hours a day. We were totally involved in sexuality. And we were doing everything together. Patti was working in the sexuality field. We ran a group together. Lectured together. And she started a book on liberated education, a book whose title I gave her and got her started on.

I had certain very proscribed views of what I would accept as valid in group sex. We decided we would make approaches to people we cared about, and we would be very straight about it. I took the gentleman's view—you pick. Patti picked people she was interested in. She would come in and say, "This woman is very lusty, I'm sure you'll really like her." That meant she dug the guy.

It was really great. People would come over for dinner and we would propose group sex or lead to it. We'd make funny little remarks about having this gigantic tub in the back. It seemed to me everybody was making it in group sex. Obviously, everybody *is* into it, on one unconscious level or another.

So a couple would come over and we'd have dinner and drink a couple of glasses of wine, go up to the bedroom and put on music, turn the lights low and smoke a joint; sometimes put on a candle, build a fire, build a whole scene. I have a bedroom that was built for group sex. It has just one gigantic bed. I liked the experience that the whole night would be a focused, intensive occasion for sexual feelings. It's incredible to watch bodies moving and screwing around. People screwing are beautiful. I really enjoyed Patti being totally turned on and being able to follow herself and go where she wants to go and not being hassled by it. I very much enjoyed choreography, developing sexual ballets.

The other great experience was looking at some guy screwing and say, "Jesus Christ, his butt goes up and down just like mine. There's really no difference." When Patti was screwing Walter, Walter would screw for an hour at a time and just pump away. Patti liked that a lot. I didn't think that she was having a better time than with me. She was having a different time. It didn't really apply to me. There really is no magic. They screw their way, but they all screw the same. Some people are taller, blonder, what else is there? Richer, younger, bigger cocks, I don't know. They're not me. There were times when four of us were screwing that I was a little uptight. It's hard to explain, but I was always concerned that Patti did not get envious—not jealous, envious. I didn't want her to see me having a better time than she was having. Envy is a weight that makes people kill the other person. I didn't want her to kill me.

Rebecca was always a part of it. Patti and I alternated who got up with her every morning when we weren't with any particular group. Before she would go to bed, she would ask, "Who do I get up in the morning with?" That simple. We always arranged it that whichever parent—Patti or I— was on duty that morning would be the one taking the master bedroom. So Rebecca went to the master bedroom. If there was a different mate there, that was fine: It would be people she knew. We never had a scene where she would wake up and there would be a strange person in bed. I always demanded that the other couple relate to Rebecca in one way or another.

I was into scheduling a different couple seven days a week, so it would be almost total anonymity. I really wanted a satiable time. I would just as soon have gone to a singles bar. I really wanted just to keep Patti in a whirl. But she was always trying to fall in love with somebody. That's the short and long of it in terms of why group sex became increasingly uncomfortable. Patti would always fall in love, which was not part of the deal we had made. I mean, friendships, OK, but Patti would always fall in love because that is her way of getting people to love her. I remember after one of our early group-sex scenes, Patti began to cry because this guy wasn't responsive enough to her. We were taking a bath. And she confronted me that she was a little girl who had to be loved. She didn't love him but she needed this kind of "I love you, I will give you everything, I will totally focus on you." It really cut me out. Those were bad scenes.

I remember we went to see the big-time porno film, Marlon Brando's *Last Tango in Paris*, and had a big fight about it. I think it was a very significant film, a really funny turn-on film. Patti saw it as an exploitation of women. I saw Brando as reality and the little chippie as romanticism, the romantics of the world destroying people all around them because romantics cannot deal with reality. I was really saying to Patti, "That's where you are." Those were the kinds of fights we were having. Very painful for Patti. Very irritating for me.

My attorney introduced Patti and me to another couple at his house, saying, "Here are two people that you would like as friends." They seemed like a perfectly nice couple. We were in different fields and that was stimulating. I found her physically attractive and I was delighted Patti found him attractive. I remember calling up my attorney's wife—his wife is very conventional middle-class Jewish and he's kind of an uptight guy—I loved calling them and saying, "You were very right. We liked the Hendersons very much. In fact, we're marrying them!"

Patti had come up with the idea that we all should live

with each other and have a foursome marriage. There was the sense of each of us growing and learning about each other. It would be a new experience for me. We would have an extended family. All four of us were there. That was the spot in time we were at, and a group marriage was the way that we could bring that moment to its fulfillment. It was an intense experience for me and that was fine.

We had a public engagement party announcing that the four of us were going to make it a foursome—a group-marriage engagement party. There were twenty to thirty people at the party. Most of the guests were really turned on by the idea. After five or six sociological and emotional questions, they'd ask about the parameters of group sex. My response was generally, "I can understand your curiosity. Try it. If you don't want to try it, anything you could imagine is possible. Your scene would be your scene."

The foursome split a few weeks after the engagement party. We began to draw up a group-marriage contract, and we couldn't agree on details. First, the minimum condition for us working was the four of us staying together. The other guy wouldn't give up his fucking house in Palo Alto. Second, we would have to have regular, ongoing foursome discussions which were focused on the foursome relationship. Finally, whether we liked it or not, we had to learn to fuck foursome because anything other than that would be a sure way to sexual jealousy.

I also felt that we had to have certain protections built in. I wanted a prenegotiated, signed separation agreement with terms of separation so that we wouldn't be forced to stay together. I think that's absolutely essential. But it fell apart largely because the other guy would not make the commitment with Patti. There were awful moments with the four of us sitting around the table and Patti standing behind him and fondling him as he's saying to his wife, "I don't want anything but to go back with you. I don't want any of this." Saying it right in front of Patti! I said to him,

"Your wife wants me and my wife wants you. You've been chosen. Why do you feel that every choice has to be yours?" Finally, Patti pulled him out of the foursome to get him. And that was the end. Marilyn stayed on and Patti is still trying to be with the other man. I think she feels that she got out on a limb and made a mistake.

I think I anticipated everything that occurred between Patti and me except for one experience. I never predicted her totally bitter, destructive attack on me. The day after my fiftieth birthday, somebody rang the bell and I was handed a divorce summons. I found out I was being divorced because I was cruel and I beat her up. I maimed her and forced her into unnatural sexual acts. Ugh! The worst kind of incredibly sick divorce.

But I have no regrets. They were good years. And I think we both made the most of that time. Both Patti and I got a great deal out of it. We were able to expand each other and ourselves. We each had another person, a teacher, a mentor, in those areas that were difficult for each of us to expand in. Patti now teaches a course I designed at San Francisco State. It's called "Marriage and Its Alternatives."

Patricia Manning works in San Francisco as a psychotherapist, lecturer, author, and child day-care organizer. Voluptuous and striking at thirty-one, she lives in a large San Francisco apartment near her former husband and shares the care of their daughter with him. Ms. Manning is a warm but reserved talker.

PATTI:

I knew who John was before I met him. I had heard his name and I knew that he was the head of my seminar on child development. So before I even saw him, I was attracted to this aura about him. At the time, I was married and living in Minneapolis, but I was attending this post-graduate training conference in Pittsburgh.

So here I was, married for a very short time, like six months, and I can't say I really was in love with my first husband. It had been like a Minneapolis thing. I was the oldest unmarried around—twenty-one—so I simply looked around and chose the most eligible of the men I was seeing and married him. He was a salesman for Ralston-Purina at the time and part of his chart was to later become a stock-broker, which he did. I knew eventually he would make $25,000 and I would become a country club leader.

Well, one night at this conference in Pittsburgh I went up to John and said that my friend and I wanted to go to Daly's that night and he offered to take us both. And then after Daly's he devised a way to get me into bed and my friend not, and so we started our affair.

It was a whole new experience to be with him, and I loved it. I'm admitting now to a lot of things that I wouldn't have then, like being from Minnesota and being star-struck. I was very, very impressed with him and impressed with myself for being with him. Also, John was quite good sexually and I was relatively inexperienced. My husband was good at hearty lovemaking and he served me well, but this was a whole new experience for me. John called me the first morning I was back at work in Minneapolis and said he was very struck. This thing between us, John and me, was something very out of the ordinary. He said we had to get together and I said, "Yes, I felt the same way." We made plans to get together, once in San Francisco, once in Pittsburgh, you know, and eventually I told my husband that I wanted a divorce. I didn't say anything about John. But by then I was madly in love with him. We had met in June and on August 29 I was on a plane to live in San Francisco.

Being with John was like a romantic narcotic, an escape from my old world. I transcended my environmental boundaries and my natural ones. John is twenty years older than I am; he was working for civil rights in the South while I was still dancing at the University of Minnesota. He was surrounded by star-quality people I was very impressed by. You know, people who have radical credentials but have been out of civil rights for some time and now have very luxurious life-styles. But I was very impressed.

From the start we spent most of our time in bed talking, mostly him telling stories to me. I was fascinated by this totally different world. He told me about civil rights and Italian weddings and San Francisco and it was all just incredible to me. I was pleased that he was taken with me and my remarks and comments. I guess psychologically I wanted to be someone different from what I was and he thought I was good material and wanted to help me do that. John has a personality that can't really resist a fan. And for him I was this package of someone who was young and smart and pretty and also he liked that I was a WASP—he really knew nothing about my family in Minneapolis but he made up this whole trip where we were something just under the Rockefellers.

Now, John and his second wife had been married for fourteen years and were fighting a lot and at this point John was just exhausted by it. That kind of relationship wouldn't have been acceptable for either of us. I could never be a yes-person for anyone. I thought I would always work on my own without his help, always be my own person. I never even wanted to take his name. We both saw this thing as a way to grow.

But I just wasn't adjusted to living openly with a man at the time. I wanted the freedom to do and be everything, but I couldn't do it without the marriage license. I didn't want anybody to say I was just John's wife, but on the other hand, I could always say whose wife I was. And as soon as we got married, we were much more open as a couple. We loved having people come over and kind of celebrate with us our "coupleness." Our life was very exciting. It was wonderful to have somebody interesting to talk to. You know, somebody you could just feel you could tell any kind of thought. We liked to just bat ideas around all the time. I got a job as a social worker in the Headstart program and I worked with Chicanos and Italians. All I knew about Italians in Minneapolis was that they ate spaghetti. The whole world of San Francisco and John was new and exciting. It just bowled me over.

At the start, we didn't have any sexual problem. John was gentle, more experienced sexually, and it was very pleasing for both of us. But then, right after we were married, I had what he called an affair—it was just a one-night stand—and John went bananas over that. I couldn't stand it. I said, "Okay. I can't take the fighting. I'm leaving." Next thing I know, we're into marriage counselors, his friends. I didn't want to go into therapy with John at that time. It was too much like being spanked. Those good doctors couldn't do a thing for me. But I had one friend who I trusted, a woman. She talked to me about what I really wanted, and I wanted to be married to John, but I hadn't been with as many men as I would have liked. I had this fantasy of screwing around. My friend told me that she had tried that and ended up going back to her husband. She said it wasn't all that romantic. In fact, it was a pretty shitty way to live. I was distressed. I certainly didn't want to repeat my first marriage. After talking with my friend, I went back to John with the determination to stay.

But another thing that really kind of screwed us from the side is that I learned from this older woman friend of John's that he slept with his ex-wife one time when he went back to drop off the children. I felt very threatened by his ex-wife. I remember feeling that he could do this and I would never find out. I could fuck up, but when he did that

I would never know, and he would be seeing her every weekend for the rest of our lives. There developed this undercurrent of not being able to trust. But I wanted to be married to John and we knew we had to work something out.

So what happened is I got pregnant. The seal. I started really getting into my own body. It's so wonderful walking around and feeling it move, right here by your crotch. It was a very sensual time for me. I would buy bikini underpants to wear under my belly and look at myself in the mirror. I just loved my body. But John stopped screwing me about three months before Rebecca was born because she would kick him and he couldn't stand it. I was going up the wall. And I suspect he was a bit turned off by it all, that I could be so turned on just by what was happening in my body.

When we had the baby, she looked like the most fantastic thing in the world. And that began three months of solid soul and body contact and I was crazy about it. Those were good times all around for both of us. But it was also a case of a new mother getting abandoned in a way. I really adored Rebecca much more than her father could. It wasn't his fault completely, but I really felt he ran out on me. It was natural childbirth and he was supposed to be there with me. I gave birth hours before I was supposed to and the hospital had sent him home. But I still felt he should have been there. He was there a half hour after she was born and then he went away again.

Corny as it sounds, the childbirth thing felt absolutely, clearly, my own thing. And it also was for me the beginning of the Women's Movement. A friend of mine from work called and said, "Well, what is it?" and I said, "A girl." And he said, "Well, John's disappointed, I'm sure, but he'll get over it." I didn't know what he meant. I had just not thought that it was better to have a boy. And for me that was the start of the whole thing. Before then, I had heard about the Women's Movement, but I thought it was obviously dykes and I wasn't interested. I had even thought that if John could go into consciousness raising with me, it would be OK. But now I got very, very involved and I joined a CR group. That was another thing that separated me from John. Other than giving me some sperm, he had nothing whatever to do with the baby. And clearly, he could have nothing to do with the movement. Things changed. My ideas about the relationship changed a lot. We had a lot of fights, especially about child care and how to divide it up, because I wanted to. He felt he worked and made more money. You know, all the old arguments. Up to that point, it had been a very traditional marriage. More than I had realized. I did the cooking and the cleaning. It took seven months of hair-raising fights to get him to change. Now he considers himself quite liberated.

For a while there, this new life went both ways with John. There was a transition time in which it was very stimulating for him. It took a while before it hit the home front, like child-care issues and so on. But he eventually adjusted to that. I'll tell you, I think the real downfall was the separate personality I developed; I was changing so that I didn't always look to him for how things should be, whether it was political opinions or opinions of people or whatever. He was basically right back to where he was with his first wife. They had spent most of their time hassling about power and now we were doing the same. Our relationship began not to work. If I would do something independently, he would put me down. He began to get impotent. He hadn't yet worked things out for himself—that someone can love him if he doesn't control them. I wasn't thinking less of him at that time. I just felt so much better about myself that I really felt I was more loving.

Around that time I went back to work and I started having a little affair. I didn't tell John about it then, only that I was having fantasies about other men and I was very upset about it. I didn't want any behind-the-scenes affair right then. Although it felt good, it took away from working our way through the bad things that were happening in our marriage. So we decided to work out some sort of new program.

Our sex had dwindled off to nothing. We had always got on together well if he was teaching me something. So while he was helping me become aggressive, I was fine. But after I became that, we were at a shaky point again. John is a very programmed personality. He would have a tendency to map out what it was we would be doing sexually. It's like, "Now, why don't you be aggressive and then I'll turn you over and ta ta ta ta ta." I had learned how to do almost everything, and felt comfortable, then I just liked to let it happen and I happened to still like to spend about 50 percent of the time flat on my back. We would rehash afterward. Of course. Talk. Talk. Talk. Talk. We talked everything to death. It's like every time we would get into bed, he would want to hear every detail of what I had done that day—at work and meetings—and he would give me the diagnostic wrap-up on it. He could give a diagnostic wrap-up on anything.

So we had to find something else to keep us going. At that time I seemed to think that I had a minimum daily requirement of one orgasm and John was intentionally trying to drive me crazy by only screwing me every other week or so. So we came up with a new program: group sex. It was based on not trusting each other and not really being satisfied, not being able to transcend in our sexual relationship . . . you know, the kind of hassle that was going on about my growing. So we decided that somehow by trying this, it would become like a stimulus. I mean, it *is* such a unique way to live. It's like having a child or buying a house. It was our new occupation. And I'll tell you, it was a good time for me. I remember feeling very pretty, generally high.

It was a fairly obsessional year. We did a lot of recruiting by asking friends that we were attracted to if they were interested. Some people were quite horrified. But after a while your skin gets a little toughened. It took courage, 'cause I knew in some way it wasn't acceptable. And in some ways it was always hard. Like I could have a great time sexually with another man but that meant having my husband with another woman under my eyes. I loved the sex, but the whole experience was very bittersweet because I think that I can be possessive. But I'll tell you, John and I were sleeping with each other much more. Most of the time it worked out fairly. John could state an individual preference for a woman, but it was understood that I was not going to offer up my body in order that he be able to sleep with some guy's wife. And of course, afterward, we'd compare notes. How much he enjoyed it, and how much I did.

Midway in this new marriage arrangement of ours, I made a trip to Minneapolis with Rebecca. John and I had talked about having separate affairs and decided that that was permissible. Well, I went there, and you know, I met a man and realized that I could take pleasure in *not* having an affair. To be able to have a choice and to say no. And then I got back home and John was late picking me up at the airport because he had made a choice to have a new "anyone" while I was gone. I was just livid! John had also invited his new friend and her husband to come to the country house that weekend. I was just very angry that she and John were trying to get me together with her husband. I wouldn't have anything to do with it. But then, it was maybe three weeks later, John wanted to invite them over for dinner and I decided to sleep with them. I think a lot of that was just topping John. Sometimes John would get jealous but he would also say that it turned him on. I think it did turn him on to see me with other men.

And then we met one couple which I fell in love with, or thought I fell in love with. And Johnny fell in love with the woman. So for a while there, it was just the four of us. We cut off all other relationships. We thought that maybe the four of us could all live together. Sexually, it was pretty good. John Spinelli was the main ringleader in the whole thing. And then we began discussing things. It took so much talking. John was making up these schedules. Like my daughter would have four parents, Marilyn would have time with her and George would have time with her. It was just weirder and weirder. It's like life has to be all work and no play. This life was going to be, just forever, an encounter!

John went so far as to have an engagement party. The people who came said it was the strangest thing, these four weird people walking around, obviously not getting along! *(laughs)*. We were all on different planes.

This other woman, Marilyn, is a liar basically. She may be the weirdest one of us all. She was like smiles all the time. In the group marriage she would always say to a person what they wanted to hear. Yes, she was another pleaser. She is very much like I was when I first married John. I went away with just Rebecca for a month that summer and all I could think about during that time was that as soon as I became me, John no longer loved me. So the person that I thought was the first person to really love me, never really met me. He loved what he had hopes of me becoming. And I think Marilyn's just starting back at the beginning again. She's just like I was. You know, basically very submissive and passive but with all the flair.

That group marriage didn't work for long. And then John moved just Marilyn in. That was the end. I felt terrible. I think that was the lowest day of my entire life.

In retrospect, I think John's and my sexual involvements were just too much. I think the only way something like that could work—and I've talked to people who have done it—is if the original couples have stability. And we had none. That's stronger than any feelings about the group marriage. Stability.

9

Real
Marriage

We came away from our interviews with a mixture of feelings. One day, we would be in utter awe of many of these couples for daring so much in their marriages. Another day, we could only think of them as spoiled children who corrupted their marriages with self-indulgence. At times we would be struck by the inevitable mess of the whole business of male-female coupling, and other times we would be convinced that each of these marriages could have been satisfying if only the partners had tried to be more compassionate with one another. Throughout, however, we found ourselves concluding that these marriages were victimized by myths. They were doomed by aspirations that made real marriage intolerable.

One of the people we interviewed said in a thoughtful moment, "You know what marriage *really* is? A lot of sitting around." The rude fact is that no matter what marriage myth a couple aspires to, no matter who they think they are, much of the time they are all Blondie and Dagwood. No matter how high they aim, the same old tensions are recycled. It is painful to acknowledge that even in the most modern marriages, women often remain locked in the role of "demander" and men in the role of "cold fish." And for every meaningful sexual, spiritual, or intellectual encounter between a husband and wife, there are still hundreds of communications on the order of, "Is now the best time for a nap?" and, "Shhh, everyone can hear you." The myths of perfect marriage do not realistically deal with the routine issues of married life, and to the couples caught up in the myths, these issues are ultimately excruciating. The older myths—the Simple Nesters and the Worshiper-Worshipee—romanticize the daily rituals of simple domesticity, glorify the everyday; and the newer myths try to cover up the routineness of married life with different kinds of excitement.

There is a Bedouin proverb that goes, "Beware of what you desire, for you will surely get it." In perfect marriage, one chases a special vision of happiness—and frequently gets it. That can be a problem. One species of happiness can crowd another out. To actually become soul mates is a wonderful thing, but when that intimacy makes talking preferable to lovemaking, the marriage can suffer. Or worse yet, once a powerful aspiration has been satisfied in a marriage, a new aspiration may suddenly seem more appealing. The spiritual life was marvelous, but now the gutsy life is essential. The original marriage has served its purpose and now it is time to start working on that next aspiration— preferably with a new partner who specializes in it.

Many perfect-marriage aspirations turn out to be short-term goals. Once satisfied, a new goal is needed. There seems to be a new marriage myth in the making here: the Serial Marriage. After a Super Achievers Marriage, we dream of a Super Erotic Marriage, and after that, it is time for a Simple Nesters Marriage. In perfect Serial Marriage, we could pick marriages the way we picked majors in school. Arthur Miller's sequence of marriage partners, from college sweetheart to Marilyn Monroe to intellectual soul mate, is very attractive indeed. But what is lost in Serial Marriage is the first premise of marriage itself: continuity.

A young woman recently ended a romance that was headed for marriage, saying, "I think we both could do better than each other."

In perfect marriage, everybody marries up. Each person chooses a mate who has the qualities he desires for his own improvement. If one thinks of himself as too "stable" and "unadventurous," he seeks a mate who is more "daring" and "spontaneous." This observation is not meant as some psychoanalytic description of how one seeks an opposite to fulfill a neurotic need; the subject is again the mythical images one learns to aspire to. Whether it is an Aries who found perfection in Cancer, or a chic and efficient debutante who is drawn to a bohemian wildman, the mythical image was there long before its fulfillment appeared on the scene. In gathering these stories, we saw this "Opposites-Attract" phenomenon operating at every conceivable level. Often two people who seemed virtually identical from the outside, considered themselves radically different from their own point of view.

But marrying one's aspirations frequently backfires. There is an ironic scenario that appears again and again in such marriages. The play begins with, for example, our debutante loving up her wildman every time he does something outrageous; he, in turn, smothers her with kisses each time she efficiently prepares an elegant supper. So far, so good—they have both found their perfect completion. But soon the wife discovers that having an eccentric husband requires her to be even *more* practical than she was when she married. Else, who will keep the household going? And her husband discovers that he must provide all the excitement in the marriage because it certainly is not coming from her. By the play's end, each mate is insisting that the other change the very qualities that were originally so attractive. Each now sees he must acquire that quality on his own. The wife in our example now finds her husband's outrageous behavior an appalling burden; she demands that he become steadier and more responsible so that she can have some room in the marriage to be a little crazy herself. And the husband finds his wife's organization of their life overwhelming; he demands that she loosen up and become more spontaneous so that he can have some room to create his own order. Ironically, each now wants the same changes—but it is too late. Their life has come to demands, to defining one another's roles, and the joy has emptied out of it. As the curtain falls, they exit in opposite directions.

One person we spoke with said, "These days when I see a woman in the street with a happy face, my first thought is not that she's just fallen in love—it's that she just got her separation papers!"

There is another new marriage myth in the air at this time: perfect divorce. That myth assures everyone they can transcend mundane married life. Perfect divorce promises deeper feelings, more fulfilling experiences, and a superior life-style; it is the ultimate self-improvement scheme.

Yes, the myth of perfect divorce is painfully reminiscent of the myths of perfect marriage. It even promises a mature and sophisticated relationship with one's mate, albeit one's former mate. But like the perfect-marriage myths, the myth of perfect divorce puts a terrible strain on real life. Knowing that a perfect divorce should be a "creative growth experience," one suffers doubly if he only happens to feel stuck and lonely and empty.

The myths of perfect marriage and perfect divorce both grow out of the same obsession: to have a higher level of experience. For most people, perfect marriage promised to avoid the banalities of their parents' marriages; perfect divorce makes the same promise. In earlier eras, marriage was a rite of passage that broke couples away from the previous generation. Now divorce is that rite. After a couple has made the depressing discovery that their perfect marriage was frustrated by the same limitations as their parents' marriages, divorce is the way they will finally break new ground.

But there may be one other option—imperfect marriage, sometimes known as real marriage. All the people in this book who sought perfection had one goal in common: to be married. There really is something remarkable in that. One cannot imagine more antithetical life-styles than, say, those of the Super Achievers and the Spiritual Couple, yet they each thought up the identical scheme for maintaining their life-styles—as man and wife. There must be something about the common denominator of marriage, about the security and continuity and the unique quality of love it can provide, that is appealing in itself, no matter how pedestrian one feels in admitting that.

In our interviews, when we asked for descriptions of the most consistent good times our perfect couples had shared, we were usually confronted by a kind of embarrassment. These good times, it seemed, were really quite ordinary. A walk in the park, a trip, an evening with friends, a warm homecoming, the birth of a child. They were not the bigger-than-life, myth-fulfilling moments after all; those moments were rare and eventually bred disaster. And while the very real, consistent, and conventional times—those times that are the special product of marital intimacy—are not enough for a perfect marriage, they *are* enough for a real marriage.

We were surprised by the attitude we found ourselves developing toward the end of our interviews. We, personally, had been as tantalized as anyone else by the hopes for marital perfection the myths had to offer; we were avid subscribers to every new marriage scheme that appeared in such books as *Open Marriage* or was romantically portrayed in films and novels. But in the end we became convinced that such schemes cannot be translated into reality. The hard fact is that marriage at its best *is* compromising. Yes, real marriage *is* a great deal of sitting around, a whole lot of

Blondie and Dagwood situations day in and day out. And as one person we interviewed admitted, monogamous sex does have a habit of trading off eroticism for familiarity, no matter how many ingenious devices one employs. Marriages through all time have been tortured by the threat or fact of infidelity, but the myth that some new kind of marriage can incorporate open infidelity simply does not turn out to be true.

There is no doubt that real marriage has less to offer most of us than it offered earlier generations. It can no longer satisfy our deepest aspirations; we aspire to much more than our parents did. But where is it written that marriage must fulfill all our deepest aspirations for life or else we should abandon it? Why do we insist on loading our marital situations—marriage *or* divorce—with more crucial expectations than we do any other enterprise in our lives?

The question of what to do with our deepest aspirations is ultimately personal; it cannot be shared perfectly with anyone. If we look for continuous excitement and surprise, if we set our sights on unlimited sexual adventure or total personal privacy, it makes no sense to burden ourselves with the real limitations of marriage. But if we aspire to the security and continuity of marriage, if we set our sights on enduring intimacy and day-to-day shared times, we can only reach for these satisfactions by first cutting ourselves loose from the myths of perfect marriage.